NO HOPELESS FUTURE

Expositions on the Book of Ruth

Dale Ralph Davis

All Scripture quotations are the author's own translation.

ISBN Nos:
Paperback: 978-1-5271-1316-9
Ebook: 978-1-5271-1404-3

Published in 2026
by
Christian Focus Publications Ltd,
Geanies House, Fearn, Ross-shire,
IV20 1TW, Scotland, UK.

www.christianfocus.com

Cover design by Daniel van Straaten

Printed by Bell & Bain, Glasgow

No Hopeless Future delivers what fans of Dale Ralph Davis expect: thoughtful, learned exposition of the scripture accompanied by engaging illustrations and heart-penetrating application. I can't imagine a better guide through the book of Ruth. The journey from Moab to Bethlehem will leave readers, like Naomi, richer for it.

Betsy Childs Howard
The Gospel Coalition

Dale Ralph Davis has a way of reading biblical texts that gets to their very heart by drawing out what's really there which you hadn't much noticed the first time around. He does it again here, beautifully, with the book of Ruth. And he does it with humanity, humility, honesty, with the skill of an expositor, the warmth of a preacher, and the gentle heart of a shepherd who loves the stories of the Bible and the God of those stories. I read this with delight and immense profit and I am sure you will too.

David Gibson
Minister, Trinity Church, Aberdeen

Whenever I start a new preaching series through a book of Scripture, I want to know if Dale Ralph Davis has written a commentary on it. He has demonstrated a pattern of insightful exegesis and compelling application in his writings, and this commentary on the book of Ruth is exactly what you would expect from him. Well written and clear and faithful, this little book by Davis is another outstanding volume. The book of Ruth tells a beautiful story of God's providence and provision, and Davis's commentary will help you see and appreciate what the biblical author has written.

Mitchell L. Chase
Pastor, Kosmosdale Baptist Church, Louisville, Kentucky

CONTENTS

Preface

I'm tempted to say that the US Marines have come through again. But that wouldn't be true. A Marine has come through, to wit, Major Timothy A. Burnam. He is the one responsible for this document you are holding in your hand.

When I was serving as pastor of Woodland Presbyterian Church in Hattiesburg, Mississippi, Timothy was a tall, slender, impish, entertaining teenager there. I preached a series on the Book of Ruth at Woodland and later (after some updating and revision) at First Presbyterian in Columbia, South Carolina. Unbeknownst to me, Major Burnam, besides doing 'full duty' with his Katie and their five children and serving in the Marines, had taken the audio recordings of the 'Ruth' series and transcribed them into written form. I'd no idea he had done this until I received the document in my 'inbox' – with a little nudge about possible publication.

Lest you think too lightly of Timothy's labors, let me begin by assuring you that I do not believe there is a purgatory. However, if there were, one form of it would consist of trying to take down in writing oral expositions of biblical texts. In the sweep and movement of hearing a sermon orally/audibly, we don't always catch the pauses, uhs, hmms, sentence fragments, and disconnections that appear in all their glaring blemishes when reduced to paper. The time and angst and patience of such a task are more than daunting. So … my immense thanks to Mr Burnam for this labor of sweat and kindness. He has done the 'dog work.'

I have lightly edited Timothy's manuscript, and I have been careful to keep the 'sermon' form. There are no footnotes. To my thinking at least, a preached sermon is different than a written composition. So you will likely find these expositions have more of an 'informality,' with the use of contractions and direct address. Imagine you are hearing rather than reading them.

I would probably never have tried to publish this material, but, given Major Burnam's 'push,' I could not allow all his fine work to go to waste.

Dale Ralph Davis
Advent 2024

1 THE LORD WHO TAKES AWAY AND GIVES (Ruth 1)

(1) In the days when the judges ruled, a famine came on the land, and a man from Bethlehem-judah went to stay a while in the country of Moab – he, his wife, and his two sons.

(2) The man's name was Elimelech, his wife's name Naomi, and the names of his two sons, Mahlon and Chilion, Ephrathites from Bethlehem-judah; when they came to the country of Moab, they stayed there.

(3) Then Elimelech, Naomi's husband, died, so she was left along with her two sons.

(4) Now they took for themselves wives, Moabite girls; the name of the one was Orpah, and the name of the second Ruth. And they lived there about ten years.

(5) Then even the two of them, Mahlon and Chilion, died, so that the woman was left without her two children and without her husband.

(6) Then she rose up, along with her daughters-in-law, and returned from the country of Moab, because she had heard that Yahweh had looked after his people by giving them food.

(7) She went forth from the place where she was – her two daughters-in-law with her, and they went on the road to return to the land of Judah.

(8) And Naomi said to both her daughters-in-law: 'Go on, turn back, each to the house of her mother. May Yahweh deal kindly with you, as you have done with the dead and with me.

(9) May Yahweh grant that you find a secure place, each in the house of her husband.' Then she kissed them, and they lifted up their voice and wept.

(10) And they said to her, 'But we're going to return with you to your people.'

(11) Then Naomi said, 'Go back, my daughters! Why will you go with me? Do I still have sons in my womb that they might become your husbands?

(12) Turn back, my daughters, go on, for I am too old to have a husband. If I should say, "There's hope for me," even if I had a husband this very night, and even if I gave birth to sons,

(13) would you therefore wait until they grew up? Would you therefore hold yourselves back from having husbands? No, my daughters, for it is far more bitter for me than for you; indeed, the hand of Yahweh has gone forth against me.'

(14) And they lifted up their voice and wept again. Then Orpah kissed her mother-in-law, but Ruth clung to her.

(15) And she said, 'Look, your sister-in-law has gone back to her people and to her gods; go back after your sister-in-law.'

(16) Then Ruth said, 'Don't pressure me to abandon you, to turn back from following you, for wherever you go, I will go, and wherever you lodge, I will lodge; your people will be my people, and your God, my God.

(17) Wherever you die, I will die, and there I will be buried. May Yahweh bring all the more disaster on me if even death separates me from you.'

(18) When Naomi saw that she was dead set on going with her, she stopped speaking to her about it.

(19) So the two of them went on until they came to Bethlehem. When they entered Bethlehem, the whole town was in a stir over them. The women said, 'Is this Naomi?'

(20) And she said to them, 'Don't call me Naomi; call me Mara, for the Almighty has deeply marred me.

(21) I went away full, but Yahweh has brought me back empty. Why will you call me Naomi, since Yahweh has testified against me, and the Almighty has brought disaster on me?'

(22) So Naomi returned, and Ruth the Moabitess, her daughter-in-law, with her, who returned from the country of Moab. And they came to Bethlehem at the beginning of barley harvest.

This passage could almost be a newspaper account, couldn't it? Verses 1-5 present 'just the facts,' but not without a touch of sympathy. It's a story of multiple adversities.

This family from Bethlehem-judah, due to the pressure of a famine, goes to Moab. While we don't have a huge map here at the pulpit, you might find a small one in the back of your Bible. Bethlehem-judah is about six miles south-southwest of Jerusalem. I'm guessing Elimelech and his family traveled northeast, around the north end of the Dead Sea, then went south until they reached Moab.

Verses 1 and 2 describe this *big move*. Then verse 3 presents a *hard fact*: Elimelech died. This is too soon followed by the *double deaths* in verse 5: Mahlon and Chilion, Naomi's sons, also died. Then we meet the *sad verb* in the repeated clause, 'and she was left' (vv. 3, 5).

We see a woman who considers herself too old to remarry, perhaps in her mid to late forties? Her sons have died. She has no heir, no husband, no sons. She has no one apparently to care for her in her advancing years, and her family is at risk of going extinct in Israel.

Then comes the *major decision* in verse 6: having heard that the famine in Judah was over, she decides to return. This 'return' becomes the focus of the chapter. Most all of chapter 1 depicts a scene on the road, with Naomi and her daughters-in-law beginning their journey back to Judah.

The book of Ruth is, for me, a frightening book. There are two books that particularly unsettle me in the Old Testament: Job and Ruth. You see, verses 1-5 here show how quickly your life can fall apart. Well, you can do the math: one famine, three deaths, ten years, five verses.

However, as we examine this passage that tells us what the Lord has taken away, I believe the testimony is not entirely negative. The book of Ruth seems to be saying that the Lord who takes away also gives. The question then becomes: what does he give?

Unremarkable Provision

Well, in the first place, he gives unremarkable provision. Consider verse 6 in light of verse 5: 'Then she rose up along with her daughters-in-law and returned from the country of Moab, because she had heard in the country of Moab that Yahweh had looked after his people by giving them food.'

There was famine, which was why they had originally gone to Moab to sojourn there. And now there's provision. The famine is over.

Yahweh has looked after his people by giving them food. This is one of the two texts in the book that speaks of Yahweh's direct activity – chapter 1, verse 6, and chapter 4, verse 13. In other places, the work of Yahweh is more subtle. But here's a direct action, you might say, by Yahweh.

We call this 'unremarkable provision' because we usually don't think too much about this kind of provision (at least not in the west). Now, this doesn't relieve Naomi's poverty, and it doesn't take away her sorrow, does it? But it does show that the God who brings famine also brings relief from famine. It's evidence of Psalm 111: 'He provides food for those who fear him. He is ever mindful of his covenant.'

So what do you have here? You have two facts: Naomi has terrible trouble, and she has daily bread. Those two things coexist.

This reminds me of the situation with our garbage. I don't know how your garbage is taken care of where you live. In our neighborhood, the garbage truck backs up to the portable dumpster the city gives us to use. At least one fellow puts it next to the back of the garbage truck, then it lifts it up, dumps the contents, and puts it back down near the curb (kerb). In other places, a garbage truck will pull up and use a robotic arm to hug the dumpster, pick it up, empty it, and put it back down. No assistance needed – just a driver.

It varies, of course. They were just about to implement, I think, that robotic system when we were leaving Hattiesburg, Mississippi a few years ago. Before that, they had always done it by hand – one or two men on the back of the truck grabbing and emptying the garbage cans into the truck. Because of how they handled the garbage cans, I never put my garbage containers out at the street on garbage days. It was a good way to get your garbage cans beat up, especially if they left them in the street as targets for oncoming cars. So I always took the 39-gallon black plastic bag liners out, tied them up, and put the bags at the end of the driveway. They could throw them on the truck, and I could have my garbage cans intact.

Now, you don't deal with garbage twice a week without beginning to think theologically about it. As you carry those bags down the driveway – usually at least two, sometimes three if we had had company – you might think: I have garbage. Ergo (that's Latin for 'therefore'), God is good. Because I wouldn't have garbage if God wasn't providing me with daily bread.

I call it the silent sacrament of the black plastic bags. It's unremarkable to us perhaps, but it's unremarkable *provision*. Sometimes you can miss that in the midst of your trouble, when all of life seems to cave in and it seems like the Lord is even against you. Sometimes you have to remind yourself: I am in deep water. But what is this? I have daily bread. Unremarkable provision.

Uncompromising Steadfastness

Secondly, the Lord gives uncompromising steadfastness. What I'm going to argue here is that Naomi remains steadfast in this trial. How does she do so? Ultimately, she gets that uncompromising steadfastness because God enables her to stand.

Let's examine this. Notice her convictions, especially in verses 13, 20, and 21. You remember how she said to her daughters-in-law in the last part of verse 13, 'It is far more bitter for me than for you; indeed, the hand of Yahweh has gone forth against me.'

I know there are differences in translations, but the last part stands pretty solid: 'The hand of Yahweh has gone forth against me.' Then notice in verses 20 and 21, when she gets back to Bethlehem at the city gate and the women are fluttering around her, she says: Don't call me Naomi. Don't call me 'pleasant.' Call me Mara, bitter.

There is a little wordplay in Hebrew that I've tried to paraphrase: 'Call me Mara, for the Almighty has deeply marred me.' Then note verse 21, 'The Almighty has brought disaster on me.'

As far as Naomi's convictions go, she thinks God is in charge here. She thinks God must, by definition, be sovereign. And she can't get away from that. If Ephesians 1:11 had been written by her time, Naomi would have agreed with it – that God is the one who works all things according to the counsel of his will.

If he's sovereign, and if part of that sovereignty involves bringing trouble into her life, that's going to mean that the sovereign God is also a mysterious and perplexing God. I think that the more you believe in a sovereign God, the more perplexities and mysteries you'll encounter. And Naomi also says, 'Yahweh has testified against me.' We'll come back to that in a moment.

So she sees Yahweh as utterly sovereign and in supreme control here. At the same time, notice that in verses 8 and 9 there's a different undertone or sentiment. You notice that's where she utters a blessing on her daughters-in-law and tells them to turn back.

Verse 8 says, 'May Yahweh deal kindly with you.' Now that's the word *hesed* – may he do *hesed*, that is, faithful love; we might render it, 'May Yahweh deal in a *hesed*-way with you, as you've done with the dead and with me.'

And then, in verse 9, she says, 'May Yahweh grant that you find a secure place, each in the house of her husband.'

Do you see Naomi's balance here? Does she like what Yahweh has done? No – he has 'deeply marred' me, he has 'brought disaster on me.' But don't you see? She doesn't think that God is only the sauerkraut on the crud of life. It's not an unbalanced, not an unhinged, view. She also knows that Yahweh is the God who deals in a *hesed*-way with people, kindly and graciously.

This is what she expresses and asks for her daughters-in-law as they go back to Moab. She doesn't say, 'May Chemosh deal kindly with you' – the so-called deity of Moab. No, she expects Yahweh to be active in blessing them, even in Moab.

That's interesting. She doesn't have this one-sided view of the Lord, as if he is just rubbing her nose in the grit and the grime. But she sees and admits that along with placing her in this trouble he also deals kindly with people. There's such a balance here, even in her distress.

Let's come back to what we mentioned earlier – she also has a consciousness that she is in the wrong. She thinks she is, anyway. This appears in her assertion that 'Yahweh has testified against me' (v. 21). Again, some of your translations may not read that way, but I think that is the better rendering here. What the Lord has done shows that, in some way, she is or has been in the wrong. She seems to think that the Lord, by these actions and experiences and trouble, shows that he is displeased with her. She may be right or she may be wrong about that.

But this is her view of it. However, you know how it is sometimes when you meet reverses and how you begin to think and wonder about how God may be chastising you. And it doesn't take too much effort to dredge up certain items that you think might be the explanation for why he's dealing that way with you. Your conscience gets scoured and you find yourself pondering what God may be disciplining you for. You may be right or wrong, but that happens.

Now there are some expositors who think, Yes, Naomi was right. The Lord was testifying against her. There are some expositors of Ruth who are quite certain that what you have in verses 1-5 was wrong. And perhaps that is one of the matters Naomi considered. It might be that she thought, 'Well, maybe we shouldn't have gone to Moab.'

Was that a move of wisdom or was that a failure of trust? It's hard to tell sometimes, isn't it? And what about those marriages to Moabite girls? Some expositors jump on that as well. Actually, Israel was forbidden to marry a raft of pagans, but Deuteronomy 7 doesn't say anything specifically about Moabites. But it's a debated matter. Sometimes some expositors will say, 'No, the writer wants you to see that these were wrong moves that were made.'

I can't follow that (particularly about the move to Moab) because the writer doesn't expressly criticize that. He doesn't really comment on whether that was a wrong move on Elimelech and Naomi's part. Some people will say, 'Oh, yes, but because of the way he describes it, we think that he's being negative about going to Moab.'

Well, it may be, but it's hard to know what a biblical writer thinks if he doesn't explicitly tell you what he thinks. So I don't think that we can make much out of that. I tend to think Naomi has this very natural way of thinking, that the Lord must be very displeased because of something, and she may be right or wrong about that. Instead, let's leave that debate behind. I want you to see her convictions. I think you could sum up Naomi's faith or her 'theology' here in three different propositions:

1. Yahweh is the only sovereign God. He is in charge here.
2. Yahweh is a *hesed*-showing God, or a *hesed*-doing God (vv. 8-9).
3. Yahweh has decimated my life.

Now, that kind of sums up her convictions. What I want you to see is that there's a sense in which there is a real steadfastness here. An uncompromising steadfastness.

In what way? Well, as someone has said, she complains about what God has done, but she does not deny him. She does not forsake him. Granted, she's not 'victorious,' as some people may wish. She didn't go around before she ate her breakfast singing two stanzas of 'Faith Is the Victory' or something like that. She wasn't confident or buoyant here. She complains, but by that complaint, she shows she is *still dealing with her God*. She struggles and wrestles with this God. She laments what he has done, but she does not abandon him.

Uncompromising steadfastness; we've a word for that – faith. Let me give you a couple of scenarios that may give us a handle on this kind of thing.

I remember a time in our first pastorate; we were doing a Bible study on Sunday evenings on 1 and 2 Samuel. I don't recall what the text was that we were dealing with one night, but it was one that stressed the sovereignty of God and his supremacy in all things and matters. So I was trying to press that home from the text.

In our little Sunday evening Bible study, there was a retired Presbyterian minister who attended the church. He said, 'Well, I don't agree with that. Now, for instance, when I was serving in World War II in the Pacific as a chaplain, if word had come back to my wife that I had been killed, I would hope she would not say or think, "God has brought this about," or "The Lord is behind this." I would hope she would say "it just happened."'

Now that's an interesting take because it gets God off the hook. It's also a step into paganism, because he was essentially saying: there is a God who is semi-sovereign over good things as we define good; and then there's this other factor called chance which means that some things 'just happen.' That's not a biblical position; that's not where Naomi was.

On the other hand, I remember a time in the mid-70s when I went up to relieve my sister-in-law for a while, who was taking care of my parents. I went up into Pennsylvania to help out. My mother was in the hospital at the time, I believe with a broken leg. So I was staying with my dad.

During this time, I recall one evening after we had had family worship, as we always called it. We were up in Pop's study on the second floor. Pop read a passage of scripture and then prayed.

After that – you have to understand that my father was not one who, well, he didn't put a bowl out there and spill his psychological guts and say, 'Now, look at that!' He played things pretty close to the chest. Lots of times you didn't know what he was thinking.

But it came out after prayer. It was one of those reflective moments. And he just said, 'It seems that the hand of the Lord has gone out against us lately.' A Naomi moment.

Being a perfectly healthy fellow in my early 30s, I immediately tended to think that I needed to 'defend' the Lord a little bit or something like that. You know the kind of things you think of saying. And I remember that I was all ready to say, 'Pop, when you get to be seventy-six years old, you can't expect that you're just going to have unbroken good health all the time,' etc., etc. I had some cogent secular arguments to bring.

Fortunately, I kept my mouth shut. And I'm glad, because he was right where he needed to be. It was as if he took a quote right out of verse 13 and he didn't need my help. He was dealing with his God. And you don't have to worry too much about people like that. An uncompromising steadfastness, even in the middle of that kind of trouble.

Unexplainable Faith

Now, thirdly, the Lord gives unexplainable faith in verses 16-17, in Ruth's words to Naomi. These are the very first words that Ruth speaks. She figures in the story before this, but this is the first time she talks.

What I'm going to argue here is that, looking at verses 16 and 17 in their context, you have to assume that faith is a supernatural gift from God, for there is no other explanation for it here. You notice those words:

Ruth said, 'Don't pressure me to abandon you, to turn back from following you. For wherever you go, I will go. And wherever you lodge, I will lodge. Your people will be my people, and your God, my God. Wherever you die, I will die, and there I will be buried. May Yahweh bring all the more disaster on me if even death separates me from you.'

Now Naomi had just set out her argument in verses 11 to 13. It was an argument that carried things to the point of absurdity to make its point. You remember how she said, in essence, 'Look, girls, you've got nothing. You've got no future with me. Even if I said I have a husband tonight, even if I married, even if I conceived, even if I bore sons, are you going to wait until they're grown so they can be your husbands?' 'I've got nothing I can give you.' That was her argument.

And so Orpah in verse 14, without blame, took the only rational response and returned home. But Ruth had this 'cling' thing and so she didn't. And so you have these words in verses 16 and 17.

But how is this such an unexplainable faith? Because there were no advantages whatsoever for Ruth to come to this faith and to make this kind of commitment. There's no rational basis to it, you might say. For example …

1. There was no *economic* advantage. She was going to be connecting with a widow. In that time and situation, there were no pensions. To be a widow was synonymous with destitution normally. When Ruth commits herself to Naomi, she's automatically giving herself up to a life of probable poverty and dirt under the fingernails. You didn't go to the community college outside of Bethlehem and retool yourself and go back into the workforce as a hygienist at the local dental clinic. You couldn't do that. That just wasn't an option.

2. There was no *social* advantage. Where was Ruth's social support system? It was back in Moab with dad and mother at home. She could go back there, no doubt. That's where the social links were. That's where the support was. Sometimes that kind of connectionalism in the family could be quite tight in the ancient world. In one of the texts from several hundred years before Ruth, there's an example of two sons who were disinherited by their father. Why disinherited? Because they

moved to another town. You better think twice before you leave home, Bud!

3. There was no *racial* advantage. You notice verse 22 – she's called 'Ruth the Moabitess.' She's the girl from Moab. She doesn't 'belong', in a sense, in Israel. She's not one of them. Now, I'm not saying that the Israelites around Bethlehem radically discriminated against Moabites or anything like that. They didn't hang Moabites in effigy. But it's just that she wasn't one of them. Some of you know what that's like. We've been in situations before, even within our own country perhaps, where we just aren't 'one of the locals.'

4. There was no racial advantage and there was no apparent *religious* advantage. You might say, 'Well, surely Ruth was attracted to the faith of Yahweh by what she had heard and learned from Naomi and Elimelech in past years about Yahweh, the God of Israel.' I don't know about that.

I don't know whether that would be much of an advantage. As far as what Ruth could see, Yahweh didn't seem to treat his worshipers very well. Case in point, Naomi. In Naomi's troubles Ruth had seen more of Yahweh's scourging hand than she had of his protective wings.

5. And there was probably no *psychological* advantage either. Now I'm not denying that Naomi may have been a very attractive personality normally, perhaps warm and caring and so on. We don't know exactly because that's not in the text. But we do know that as of late Naomi was probably not in the best form. She didn't, after the third death, gather Orpah and Ruth together and say, 'Now, girls, we've just had a third tragedy and death here, but let's just gather together and sing the hundred and third psalm.'

No, she didn't do that. Naomi didn't go around with that 'Fixodent' smile on her face, like some say we should, and say she's 'just praising the Lord' because the three people that matter most to her are buried under Moabite dirt. No, she didn't do that. She wasn't the most 'victorious,' winsome sort of personality at this time. There's no apparent psychological advantage that we can see here.

Of course, someone may say, 'Oh, yes, but Ruth could stick it out with Naomi for a while, but Naomi is not going to last forever; the day is going to come when she'll kick the bucket, and Ruth can go back to Moab and to her family.' No, no, you didn't hear Ruth in verse 17. 'Wherever you die, I will die and there I will be buried. May Yahweh bring all the more disaster on me if even death separates me from you.' No, this was a permanent affair. She went on oath in Yahweh's name in verse 17, and this was a commitment to Yahweh above all.

'Your people will be my people, and your God, my God.' This is not a sociological statement by which Ruth changes her address. This is a confession of faith for which there seems to be no earthly reason or explanation.

Sometimes things are so unlikely that it's simply hard to explain them. It's sort of like that situation with an Iranian hunter by the name of Ali. In about 1991 in Tehran, Ali was out hunting, but he came upon a snake and he took his gun and put the butt of it down right behind the snake's head. He must have been thinking he'd capture it and take it alive. And the snake – well, it curled the rest of its body around the butt of the gun and pulled the trigger with its tail and shot Ali through the head.

Now that's not likely! 'Snake kills hunter with hunter's gun.' There's something wrong with that. It's almost inexplicable.

And there's a sense in which there's an inexplicable element about this whole matter of coming to faith. Maybe you don't see it that way, but some of you know that that's the case. How do you explain it? Well, Paul tells us how you explain it in Philippians 1:29:

> To you it is given on behalf of Christ,
> not only to believe in him,
> but also to suffer for his sake.

Note what Paul is saying: 'To you it is given.' That means to be graciously given (see the Greek verb if you don't believe me), to be a gift of grace. 'To you it is graciously given on behalf of Christ, not only to believe in him, but also to suffer.' Paul is putting the stress on the suffering here. But that doesn't negate the believing. It too is 'given.'

Is faith your act? Yes, it's your response to the word and gospel of God. But if you scratch that faith a bit you begin to see: this is a gift. This came from somewhere else. That's the only explanation you can give.

Isn't this one of the grand mysteries of the kingdom of God, that you wonder how on earth you ever got into it? It's almost inexplicable. It's in hymn 469 in your Trinity Hymnal. You may remember how in that hymn it depicts coming into the kingdom of God as coming to the gospel feast. And a couple of the stanzas say:

> While all our hearts and all our songs
> join to admire the feast,
> each of us cries with thankful tongue,
> 'Lord, why was I a guest?'
>
> Why was I made to hear your voice,
> and enter while there's room,
> when thousands make a wretched choice
> and rather starve than come?

I can't explain it. You can't believe how you came to believe. Why? It's a gift. I think it was taught even in Ruth chapter 1, verses 16 and 17.

Unseen Support

Now, fourthly, notice that also the Lord gives unseen support, verses 19-22. These are the words of Naomi that we've spoken of earlier when she comes to the city gate, when she returns with Ruth. And Naomi's words to the women at the gate are both right and wrong. They're both true and false. They're both sad and perceptive. It's kind of a mixed bag as you look at them.

On the one hand, Naomi was right. 'The Almighty has deeply marred me.' That's probably right. Or verse 21, 'The Almighty has brought disaster on me.' I'm not going to debate her on that. What about 'Yahweh has testified against me'? Well, I don't know. That's the way she thinks about it. I don't know if she's right or not. I'm not smart enough to figure that out.

But she's also wrong. 'I went away full, but Yahweh has brought me back empty.' First part of verse 21 – that's wrong. She got messed up because if she would have just stuck out her elbow, she would have plunked Ruth in the solar plexus. Who's standing right beside her? 'Ruth the Moabitess, her daughter-in-law, who returned with her from the country of Moab.' There was someone; she didn't come back empty, but she couldn't see that.

This leads, I think, to a principle: Frequently, in and with affliction, Yahweh provides the means of easing the affliction. That may come through another person, as it does here. It may come through change or twists of circumstances.

It may come through the comfort of the Scriptures – or a combination of those. Let me back up again: Frequently, in and with affliction, Yahweh provides the means of easing the affliction – yet this is not seen at the time. We just don't see it because we're blind to it.

It reminds me of the story Roy Laurin tells in his expository commentary on 2 Corinthians. He said that a number of years ago there was a fellow who was working at night on a construction project. And he was working on the top of a wall several stories up. As he was working at the edge of the wall, he lost his balance and slipped. But he was able to catch a hold on the top of the wall as he fell and hang on.

Dangling there, he began screaming for help. But everybody was working. There was a myriad of mechanical sounds, riveting machines banging away and so on. Nobody could hear a cry of distress or emergency above the racket. And after a while, of course, you can only scream so long; you have to conserve strength. And then your strength begins to go because your arms grow numb. And after a bit more, your fingers just won't follow your will. And they begin to slip – as they did for this fellow, until his fingers let go.

And with a terrified yell, he fell – about three inches to some scaffolding that had been there all the time. But he couldn't see it in the dark.

Sometimes, sometimes the Lord puts scaffolding down there beneath you in your troubles. But in the darkness, you don't see it. But the Lord is that way. He tends to give you unseen support.

Now let's try to be clear on what our purpose is here. It's not to explain why bad things happen to good people. First, there are no 'good' people. I won't oppress you, but if, for example, I received what I deserve for only the sins of this past week, I would not be here right now. Now there's nothing particularly dicey about those sins, just twisted, evil motives and thoughts and anger and resentment and bitterness and idolatry and selfishness – these are the real 'bad' things. So we're not talking about bad things and 'good' people. But we have looked at bad things and God's people. Yet we don't know and we're not smart enough and we don't have enough time or context or insight to know sometimes whether bad things are really bad things or not. We don't have everything we need to evaluate it all.

No, all I want to say is that the Lord may take away, but that the Lord who takes away also gives.

2 GRACE AND BARLEY
(Ruth 2)

(1) Now Naomi had a relative of her husband's, a prominent man from the clan of Elimelech – his name was Boaz.

(2) And Ruth the Moabitess said to Naomi, 'Please let me go to the field that I may glean among the stocks of grain after whomever I may find grace.' And she said to her, 'Go, my daughter.'

(3) So she went and came and began to glean in the field after the harvesters, and she just happened to be in the portion of the field belonging to Boaz, who was from the clan of Elimelech.

(4) And – of all things! – Boaz came from Bethlehem and said to the harvesters, 'Yahweh be with you.' And they said to him, 'Yahweh bless you.'

(5) Then Boaz said to his young man who supervised the harvesters, 'To whom does this girl belong?'

(6) And the young man who supervised the harvesters answered and said, 'She's the Moabite girl who returned with Naomi from the territory of Moab,

(7) and she said, "Please let me glean and gather among the sheaves behind the harvesters"; so she came and has carried on from that time of the morning to the present – aside from staying in the shelter a little.'

(8) Then Boaz said to Ruth, 'Have you not heard, my daughter? Do not go to glean in another field, nor even pass on from this one – and so you must stick with my girls.

(9) Your eyes must be on the field where they are harvesting, and you must follow after them. Have I not commanded the young fellows not to bother you? And should you be thirsty, you're to go to the containers and drink from what the young men have drawn.'

(10) Then she fell on her face and bowed to the ground and said to him, 'Why have I found grace in your eyes to pay attention to me, when I'm a foreigner?'

(11) And Boaz answered and said to her, 'I have gotten a complete report of all you have done for your mother-in-law after the death of your husband; how you left your father and your mother and the land of your birth, and came to a people you had not known before.

(12) May Yahweh repay your work, and may your reward be full from Yahweh, the God of Israel – under whose wings you have come to take refuge.'

(13) Then she said, 'I'm finding grace in your eyes, my lord, for you have comforted me because you have spoken to the heart of your servant girl – though I will never be classed as one of your servant girls.'

(14) And Boaz said to her at mealtime, 'Come here and eat some food and dip your piece in the vinegar.' So she sat by the harvesters, and he passed her roasted grain, and she ate, was satisfied, and had some left over.

(15) When she rose to glean, Boaz commanded his young men, saying, 'Even among the sheaves let her glean, and don't criticize her,

(16) and even pull out for her some stuff from the bundles, and leave it so she can glean, and don't rebuke her.'

(17) So she gleaned in the field until evening. Then she beat out what she had gleaned, and it came to nearly an ephah of barley.

(18) And she carried it and came into the town. And her mother-in-law saw what she had gleaned; and she brought out and gave her what she had left over after being satisfied.

(19) Now her mother-in-law said to her, 'Where have you gleaned today, and where have you worked? May the one who took notice of you be blessed.' So she told her mother-in-law with whom she had worked – she said, 'The name of the man with whom I worked today was Boaz.'

(20) Then Naomi said to her daughter-in-law, 'May he be blessed by Yahweh, who has not abandoned his faithful love with the living and with the dead.' And Naomi added, 'The man's related to us – he's one of our redeemers.'

(21) Then Ruth the Moabitess said, 'He even said to me, "You must stay close to my young men until they have finished all my harvest"'

(22) And Naomi said to Ruth, her daughter-in-law, 'That's good, my daughter, that you go out with his girls – then they won't harm you in another field.'

(23) So she clung to Boaz's girls to glean until the close of barley harvest – and wheat harvest. And she stayed with her mother-in-law.

If you've ever made homemade ice cream, especially the non-electrical crank type, you know that when it gets hard to turn and when you can't turn it anymore, it's done. At that time, when I was a small lad, my father would take the paddle or the beater out of the middle of the ice cream canister. As he did, he would take a tablespoon and knock off the ice cream that was sticking to the beater back down into the canister. I was always chagrined at that, because he was very thorough. And as the youngest kid, that paddle would go into a cake pan, I would be given the tablespoon, and I would be able to eat what was still sticking to the paddle. But there was hardly anything there, because Pop was so awfully thorough.

But the farmers in Israel were commanded not to be so thorough in harvesting their grain, or their grapes, or their olives, because the sojourner, the foreigner, the orphan, the fatherless, or the widow, all of whom would likely be poor, were to be able to have an opportunity to engage in a kind of work welfare program by which they could pick up the leavings in the field. For instance, grain.

Israel's farmers (you can read it in Leviticus 19 and Deuteronomy 24) were not to harvest the grain clear to the edge of the field, but to leave some of it on the edges. If you were eating supper and you said, 'Oh, I left a sheaf of grain in the field,' don't go out after it. Don't go out and get it. Leave it there for the widow and the sojourner.

That's what we see happening in Ruth chapter 2. Most of Ruth 2 occurs in the field. We saw last week in chapter 1 that the main scene was what we could call 'on the road,' coming back to Israel from Moab. But now in Ruth 2, the main scene is 'in the field' – in the barley field. And most of the chapter consists of conversation, so we're going to have to eavesdrop.

What we want to know is what the chapter is telling us primarily about our God. And I think it's saying this: the Lord is both interesting and gracious in providing for his people. Now, that's the main thrust, but we need to pick that apart a little bit. In order to do that, let's ask the question: what then do we meet when we walk out into this barley field?

Subtle Providence

In the first place, we encounter subtle providence in verses 1 to 3. Verse 1 gives a kind of heads-up – it's the reader's edge. This is an aside to you, the reader. You need to realize that Naomi had this relative of her husband's named Boaz. He's called a prominent man, which likely means he was wealthy and had a solid character as well. The text just tells you that and leaves it.

Then everything seems to take place at Ruth's initiative. In verse 2, she asks her mother-in-law Naomi if she can go glean in the field and pick up the leavings behind the harvesters, if she can find somewhere they'll allow her to do so. She gets permission from Naomi.

In verse 3, we read: 'So she went and came and began to glean in the field after the harvesters, and she just happened to be in the portion of the field belonging to Boaz, who was from the clan of Elimelech.'

She 'just happened.' It's a statement loaded with understatement, you might say.

We need to be careful not to overread this. When the text says it 'just happened' that she was in Boaz's field, don't think that the writer of Ruth 2 believes in chance, that is, that everything happens merely by chance. Don't press his words into a philosophical statement, as if he's saying the Lord is over some things, but then chance also operates. That's not what an Israelite writer would say. He's just speaking the way Ruth would look at it at the time, or how we would view an event in a straightforward way. He's describing it as we often do. Sometimes, if you press things too far, you can distort what people mean.

There was a woman once who wanted W. C. Fields to speak at the final meeting of her garden club, but when she asked him, he declined. And she said to him, 'Well, but Mr. Fields, you do believe, don't you, in clubs for women?' And he replied, 'Certainly, but only if other means of persuasion fail.' Well, he distorted what she intended by 'clubs,' and you can distort what the writer here intends if you're trying to milk it as though he believes in chance, or something like that.

I think the writer is winking at you here, because he's already put you on notice in verse 1. 'Now, this fellow, Boaz, you need to keep your eye on him, reader.' And she 'just happened' to come into the portion of the field belonging to Boaz.

It's a subtle providence. Now, when I say 'providence,' you know what I mean. I mean that fascinating, low-key way the Lord has of caring for his people.

This is what we could call 'bump-along providence.' You might say, 'Well, I don't see much evidence of God's providence at work in my life.' I'm tempted to reply, 'Of course you don't. God is more subtle than that.' He wants you to think, search, ponder, and, as we sometimes say, exegete your circumstances. Look at them carefully and scour them a bit, so that you'll see there's been a lot of 'just happens' that will lead you to praise. Even walking into a particular barley field can be a step into providence. So here we meet a subtle providence.

Surprising Kindness

Secondly, we encounter surprising kindness in verses 4 to 13. Notice, by the way, the superb labor relations that Boaz and his harvesters seem to have in verse 4. In verses 5-7 Boaz inquires of his harvester foreman, pointing to Ruth and asking, 'To whom does this girl belong?' The foreman fills Boaz in about her.

Then Boaz addresses Ruth; their conversation begins in verses 8 and 9. Look at these verses and see what Boaz offers Ruth:

> Have you not heard, my daughter? Do not go to glean in another field, nor even pass on from this one – and so you must stick with my girls. Your eyes must be on the field where they are harvesting, and you must follow after them.

He gives her permission to work in his field. The foreman had probably already given her permission (verse 7 is a bit hard to translate), and Boaz confirms it.

Notice he says in verse 9, 'Have I not commanded the young fellows not to bother you?' This offers protection. Remember that at the very beginning of the book, it says this story took place 'in the days when the judges ruled.' Sometimes the judges didn't rule that well, and it could be chaotic. It could be rough and nasty (cf. Judg. 17–21). A girl working among harvesting girls and among harvesters in a field could be in danger. So Boaz assures her that he has guaranteed her protection.

He also provides for her, as we see at the end of verse 9: 'And should you be thirsty, you're to go to the containers and drink from what the young men have drawn.'

So he gives her permission, protection, and provision. Ruth is overwhelmed. In verse 10, she can't take it all in and asks why she's found grace before him. Boaz explains in verses 11-12. He begins by saying, 'I've gotten a complete report of all you've done for your mother-in-law after the death of your husband' (v. 11a).

Notice what all he says. He refers to her kindness: 'what you have done for your mother-in-law.' He acknowledges her sorrow: 'after the death of your husband.' He doesn't hesitate to speak of her loss. Then he speaks of her sacrifice: 'How you left your father and your mother in the land of your birth and came to a people you had not known before.' He also alludes to her probable apprehension or fear: 'You came to a people you had not known before; Israel is not your original turf; you're from Moab; you don't belong here in the same way as we Israelites do.' How well Boaz covered the waterfront of her concerns.

Notice how he describes her in verse 11 again: 'How you left your father and your mother and the land of your birth.' This is very much like Genesis 12:1 in one sense, where the Lord said to Abram (Abraham), 'Go from your country and your relatives and your father's house to a land that I will show you.' It's as if Boaz is saying Ruth is Abraham in skirts. She has done, in one sense, a very similar thing to Abraham.

This surprising kindness Boaz shows utterly overwhelms Ruth, as we see in verses 10 and 13. She falls on her face, bows to the ground, and says, 'Why have I found grace in your eyes to pay attention to me when I'm a foreigner?' And in verse 13: 'You have comforted me, and you have spoken to the heart of your servant girl.' She is just totally overwhelmed with this kindness. Kindness has a way of doing that, doesn't it?

Think of Stephen Lungu. He was a young black lad in what was formerly Rhodesia before it became Zimbabwe. He remembered growing up in a family as a six or seven-year-old, and he remembered how his father would rail at his mother because he doubted the paternity of their oldest son, Stephen himself. Stephen heard these arguments and beratings from his father, and he thought that he was responsible for his parents' marital difficulties.

Then one day, his mother took Stephen, his younger brother, and their little three-year-old sister to the market square in the village. She told them to wait at a certain place as if she was going to the restroom somewhere. She just left, abandoning them. There they were, orphaned with a vengeance, you might say.

Nobody wanted Stephen. His aunt didn't want him, but she allowed him to stay in her chicken coop. He had something like a burlap bag for a blanket. To feed himself, he discovered that white people threw food away in their garbage containers. He went down the alleyway between the more well-heeled white homes and would look in their garbage bins. He would try to find something that he wouldn't retch over – he retched over a lot of it – but he would try to find some burnt toast or something. That's how he sustained himself.

He was hanging out with some older boys around the golf club. One day, a fellow came out and looked at Stephen, asking if he wanted to caddy for him. Stephen was so proud and immediately agreed. He was only sorry that there was such a large rip in his shirt and that he was terribly dirty.

The man showed him where his clubs were. Stephen went over and grabbed the bag of clubs. He lifted them up, ready to take off, but he couldn't actually lift them. They didn't budge. He pulled on them and lifted until his eyes nearly popped, but he couldn't lift them. Finally he was able to drag them just a few paces, and then he dropped them on his toe. He howled in pain.

The man came back because his clubs weren't following him. Stephen was ready to burst into tears. Then, as Stephen recounts, 'Kindness rained down on me.' The man said, 'Oh dear boy, have I packed too many golf clubs for you? Never mind. You're a brave lad for trying. And soon you'll be big enough. Have some change anyway.' He dropped some silver coins into Stephen's hand.

Stephen recalls, 'My eyes blurred as tears of relief filled them. It was the first time a white person had ever spoken to me. I thought he was wonderful.'

Sometimes kindness, incidental as it may seem, just overwhelms you. And that's the way the kindness of Boaz overwhelmed Ruth. Surprising kindness.

It's interesting how Ruth describes this in verse 12. She says, 'You have comforted me and you have spoken to the heart of your servant girl.' Your translation might have something different, but that's a literal rendering: 'You have spoken to the heart of your servant girl.'

Interestingly, in Isaiah 40:1, those words – those verbs – are used when Yahweh tells the prophets to go preach to his people: 'Comfort, comfort my people, says your God.' And then: 'Speak to the heart of Jerusalem and cry to her that she has ended the term of her service, that her iniquity has been atoned for, that she has received from Yahweh's hand double in exchange for all her sins.'

'Comfort, comfort my people. Speak to the heart of Jerusalem.' In that setting, it's a matter of God's kindness extended in preaching to his people.

I wonder, is that such a bad application to make of this kindness we meet in the barley field? How does the Lord – or how ought the Lord – show surprising kindness to you as his people? Well, the pulpit is one place where that kindness should be heard.

Now, you have to qualify that. I know there's a sense that preaching the word of God is oftentimes a searching matter. It's an exposing matter. It ought to scour your insides, pull them out, open them up, and show yourself to you. That's what 2 Timothy 3 says: that the word of God is for correction and reproof. So there's that sense – you might say a negative side to it.

But there's also another side, and that is that anyone preaching or bringing the word of God ought to recognize that there are just a lot of Ruth clones among the people of God. I'm not just referring to women when I say Ruth clones, but that type of people who are desperately in need of some word of the Lord's kindness to bear them up in their troubles.

Although we need to be careful that we're not afraid to bring the negative, hard, searching word of God to the people of God, we also need to be careful to 'comfort, comfort my people and speak to the heart of Jerusalem.' One of the places where you ought to hear the kindness – the amazing kindness – of Yahweh your God is in the pulpit of your local church. If you don't hear it there, if it's all the searching, negative exposing of your sin but never showing you the comfort and the kindness of your God, then there's something wrong with that ministry.

I have a friend who's quite an exceptional preacher. He was telling me of preaching in a church in Texas some years ago. He said that after it was over, a lady came up to him and said, 'That was the first comforting sermon that I have ever heard preached from this pulpit.'

Now you have to be careful of what people tell you after sermons! It's a proven fact, I think, that church members can be wrong. Maybe this woman was exaggerating a bit, or maybe she hadn't listened as carefully as she should. Give her a little leeway there, but isn't it a tragic thing that that was at least her distinct impression? That's passing sad.

I hope you realize that if you're sitting under a ministry of the word somewhere, and if it's always just chewing out the saints in God's name, then there's something wrong with that ministry. It's not that God always mollycoddles you or turns a blind eye to your sinfulness, but there's a sense in which he is far kinder than Boaz and longs to 'speak to the heart' of his people. That's what the Servant of Yahweh was to do in Isaiah 50:4 – fulfilled in the Lord Jesus Christ. The Servant said that the Lord had given him a disciple's tongue to 'know how to sustain the weary with a word.' That's something you should often get when your preacher opens up God's word to you on Sunday morning. A surprising kindness.

Tangible Security

Now there's a third matter that you meet here, and that is what we could call tangible security. Let's look at verse 12 followed by verses 14 to 18. Let me try to summarize this quickly.

The fact that two women came to Bethlehem from Moab safely was something. That was no small matter at all. But more than that, Boaz says that Ruth has come to a grand protector. You notice what he says in verse 12. It's a sort of prayer that he expresses: 'May Yahweh repay your work and may your reward be full from Yahweh the God of Israel – under whose wings you have come to take refuge.' Here, he implies, is your grand protector.

You're used, of course, to that imagery, 'under his wings.' Psalm 91 speaks of it; the psalmist says, 'Under his wings you will find refuge.' David says in Psalm 63, 'You have been my help and in the shadow of your wings I will sing for joy.'

You might say, 'Well, that is figurative language; do we have to use figurative language like "under his wings," picturing a mother bird sheltering her young?' Well,

I suppose not. I suppose Boaz could have referred to Yahweh as the 'one to whom you look for his comprehensive protection and intimate security in your current existential situation.' But I'd as soon have 'under his wings.' I think you can handle the figurative language. I don't think that's such a hindrance at all.

Yahweh is her protector. Notice, however, that Boaz seeks to give Ruth a taste or a sample of what it means to be under Yahweh's wings. He gives her a taste, for instance, of his protection. You saw that in verse 9 when he said, 'Haven't I commanded the young men not to bother you?' So Yahweh is the one who protects, and Boaz protects. He's trying to reflect Yahweh's protection.

And then you notice the way in verse 14 that he supplies Ruth with sustenance. At lunchtime he says, 'Come on over here and eat some food.' She sat with the harvesters at lunch. He handed her roasted grain. This was no light thing. She ate and she carefully saved up what she had left over because her mother-in-law would need to eat that day. It was not a light matter, but Boaz provided her with sustenance.

And then there's something that Ruth didn't know until probably later – down there in verses 15 and 16. Boaz says to his harvesters, 'When you have the bundles together, pull out some of it and just kind of accidentally drop it. Leave it for her to come along and pick up.' He was really stacking the deck so Ruth would get a better 'take.' It was his way of providing for her.

What I want you to see is that Boaz not only prays that she would have the enjoyment of protection under Yahweh's wings, but he tries to give her a sense of what life under those wings is like. He tries to represent Yahweh to her in his protection and provision. He's reflecting Yahweh's character – and trying to give her a tangible security, as we said.

Southerners in the US probably don't care much about the problems northern generals had in the War Between the States. But General Grant had a problem around 1864 or so. He and General Lee and their respective troops were opposing one another around Petersburg, Virginia.

It was 1864 or early 1865, and Grant wanted to get word out to one of the generals under his command – Phil Sheridan, out in the Shenandoah Valley. He wanted him to attack Jubal Early's troops and cut off supplies to Lee's army. But Grant, in order to do that, left the front and traveled to western Virginia to sit down with Phil Sheridan and tell him exactly what he wanted him to do.

Why did he do that? They didn't have cell phones, obviously, but they did have telegraph. He could have telegraphed the war office in Washington, and they could have telegraphed to Sheridan and so passed on Grant's orders. Ah, but you see, there was a problem. Grant knew from experience what happened to his orders when they went through Washington.

General Halleck or Edwin Stanton, the Secretary of War, would sometimes nuance his orders or distort them or change them so that, when they arrived at their destination, they weren't Grant's orders. So since Grant wanted Sheridan to know what he wanted him to do, he traveled and had a face-to-face with General Sheridan, because he couldn't trust the war office to reflect his orders accurately.

But Boaz is trying to reflect Yahweh's character accurately. He is trying to give Ruth a taste of what Yahweh is really like in this security he tries to give her. And isn't that, by and large, what our calling is in this age? That we, as Yahweh's servants, seek to accurately reflect his character? We seek to give our contemporaries, whether in the office or school or at home and in a marriage, glimpses of what Yahweh is like. We should think and ask, 'How can I show them what Yahweh is like accurately? How can I give them a sample sketch of Jesus?' Isn't that what we are to be about? To give an accurate likeness of our God?

Fresh Hope

There's one more matter that we meet in the barley field, and that is fresh hope. In verses 19 to 23, we find that Ruth comes home with an ephah of barley (v. 17). An ephah of barley would be something like two-thirds or three-fifths of a bushel. That's a pretty good take for one day of just picking up the leavings in the field. Somebody had some help there!

Naomi's eyes kind of bugged when she saw that. In verse 19 she says, 'Where have you gleaned today and where have you worked? May the one who took notice of you be blessed.' This was amazing … that three-fifths of a bushel of barley would have lasted them for food for at least a week. All you need to do is borrow some goat's milk from a neighbor for a little cereal. This was very encouraging.

Now notice Naomi's response in verse 20, after Ruth had told her, 'Well, it was Boaz, it was his field in which I worked.' She said, 'May he be blessed by Yahweh, who has not abandoned his faithful love with the living and with the dead.'

There's a little bit of a question about how to translate or understand verse 20. Who is the 'who' there? Is it referring to Boaz, or is it referring to Yahweh? There's a debate about that. Some would argue that it's better to take this as referring to Boaz, and it may well be. There's some evidence for that. I still think, though, that the other option has the edge – taking the 'who' as referring to Yahweh: 'May he be blessed by Yahweh who has not abandoned his faithful love with the living and with the dead.'

Now do you see the contrast here with what Naomi said back in chapter 1, verses 20 and 21? When she comes back in chapter 1, after three funerals and a famine, and ten years in Moab, she says, 'Don't call me Naomi, call me Mara, for the Almighty has deeply marred me. I went out full, and Yahweh has brought me back empty. The Almighty has brought disaster on me.'

We said last week that if you are careful, you can even see faith in those statements, but how hard pressed she was there! Now she says, 'May he [Boaz] be blessed by Yahweh who has not abandoned his faithful love ....' What a change of attitude!

What gave her that hope? It was an ephah of barley. No, come on. Yes, it was. That's what signaled it. Sometimes it doesn't take much to restore hope. Sometimes it takes only a very incidental, small kindness to us to restore hope.

And here's a small sign that Yahweh had not forsaken her after all. Sometimes it just doesn't take that much. William Cowper, the hymn writer who drifted in and out of madness, has left us a kind of segment of his spiritual experience in one of his hymns.

It's Trinity Hymnal number 621. It's called 'Sometimes a Light Surprises the Christian While He Sings.' It's not a very 'popular' hymn, not like 'Blessed Assurance' or something you may sing relatively often. But it goes:

Sometimes a light surprises the Christian while he sings;
 it is the Lord who rises with healing in his wings:
When comforts are declining, he grants the soul again
 a season of clear shining, to cheer it after rain.

It's God's way to restore hope to his people. And how does he sometimes do it? He gives them an ephah of barley. It doesn't take much.

Here's another example: Stuart Holden was an evangelical minister, a vicar in the Church of England. He was a preacher in high demand, preaching all over Great Britain and North America at numerous conferences. He was sitting in his study one day, getting ready to go on about his 36th trip to North America; he even had his first-class steamship ticket for passage. But his wife was in hospital, having taken ill and needing surgery. Much as he wanted to go, he dared not leave his wife alone at a time like that. So he had to cancel.

Did I tell you that was in April 1912? And that the ship was the Titanic? He kept that steamship ticket, framed and on his study wall, as a sign of the Lord's goodness to him.

It doesn't take much. Sometimes an ephah of barley, sometimes a steamship ticket that reminds you of the faithfulness of God – and puts fresh heart into you.

Places are important, right? And we ought to remember them. I told some of you once about the Puritan Walter Pringle, who said that he had committed his newborn son to God at the plum tree on the north side of the garden door.

Places are important, like plum trees and barley fields. Do you suppose ... and this isn't in the text, we're just imagining. But do you suppose that maybe on their first anniversary, Ruth and Boaz went for a walk and came out and stood by that barley field? And Boaz says, 'Remember how it all started here?' And Ruth looks up at him and says, 'Yes, this is where I first felt the warmth of Yahweh's wings.'

3 COLD FEET AND REDEMPTION
(Ruth 3)

(1) Now Naomi her mother-in-law said to her, 'My daughter, shall I not seek out a home for you that it may go well with you?

(2) And now is not Boaz our relative? You were with his girls. Why, he's winnowing barley at the threshing-floor tonight!

(3) And you must wash and anoint yourself, and put on your cloak, and go down to the threshing-floor. Don't let the man know you are there until he is finished eating and drinking.

(4) When he lies down, you must note the place where he lies down, and you shall go and uncover his feet and lie down – and he will tell you what you are to do.'

(5) So she said to her, 'All that you say to me, I will do.'

(6) Then she went down to the threshing-floor, and did all that her mother-in-law had commanded her.

(7) Now Boaz ate and drank, and was in a good mood, and went to lie down at the end of the pile of grain – then she went quietly, uncovered his feet, and lay down.

(8) In the middle of the night, the man gave a start and turned over. And – why! – there was a woman lying at his feet!

(9) So he said, 'Who are you?' And she replied, 'I am Ruth, your handmaid – spread your wing over your handmaid, for you are a redeemer.'

(10) Then he said, 'May you be blessed by Yahweh, my daughter. You have made the latter kindness better than the former one, by not going after the young fellows, whether poor or rich.

(11) And now, my daughter, don't be afraid – all that you say I will do for you, for all the gate of my people knows that you are a woman of worth.

(12) And now, to be sure, I am a redeemer. But there is also a redeemer closer than I am.

(13) Spend the night here, and it shall be in the morning, if he will redeem you, fine, let him redeem; but if he does not want to redeem you, I shall redeem you, by the life of Yahweh. Lie down till morning.'

(14) So she lay down at his feet until morning, and she rose before someone could recognize his companion; and he said, 'Let no one know that a woman came to the threshing-floor.'

(15) Then he said, 'Bring the wrap you have on, and hold on to it.' So she held on to it, and he measured out six measures of barley, and placed it upon her. Then he went into the town.

(16) And she came to her mother-in-law, who said, 'Is it you, my daughter?' Then she told her all that the man had done for her,

(17) and she said, 'These six measures of barley he gave to me, for he said to me, "You must not go empty to your mother-in-law."'

(18) And she said, 'Sit tight, my daughter, until you know how the matter falls out, for the man will not rest unless he has finished the matter today.'

Sometimes we are unaware of certain odd connections. For instance, people in the United States found out ten minutes late that the Japanese had surrendered to end World War II.

It seems that the messenger boy who carried the pouch to the Swiss legation, where it was to be translated, made a U-turn on Connecticut Avenue and was stopped by a policeman. A traffic ticket, oddly enough, delayed the announcement of Japan's surrender by at least ten minutes.

We would never think of a traffic ticket and the surrender of Japan together in one breath. Simliarly, we probably wouldn't think of cold feet and redemption in the same breath, either. But there it is.

It's a very heart-of-the-story moment. I'm obviously assuming that in the latter part of verse 7 there were a couple of cold feet. And at the same time those cold feet lead to the redemption and care of Ruth and Naomi.

This is the third major scene in Ruth. We said in chapter 1 that the scene there is mainly on the road. In chapter 2, it's in the field. Now, in chapter 3, the scene is set at the threshing floor. The main thrust of Ruth chapter 3 is that the Lord works redemption with a great deal of suspense.

Now let's step back and approach this chapter by simply asking what we see here. The first matter we observe is primarily a doctrinal point, but I want you to see it first.

A Drama of God's Providence

Verses 1 to 5, verses 8, 12, and 18, reveal a drama of God's providence. Let's look at the drama first.

In verses 2 to 4, you have this bold, risky plan that Naomi hatches and tells Ruth to carry out. It was indeed fraught with all kinds of risk and carried the possibility of an unpredictable, possibly negative, response. After Boaz discovered this woman lying at his feet, what would he do? What would his reaction be? In verse 8, you don't know. It is safe to say, however, that

Boaz had never found a woman lying at his feet when he was down there sleeping and guarding his pile of barley grain. That's just not the sort of thing that happens to people.

And, apparently, it scared the liver out of him for a moment. Then, first, you don't know what his reaction to Ruth's request will be, but then, of course, there is a little more suspense, because even after Boaz said he was willing to marry Ruth and care for her, he says there is another fellow who's a closer relative than he is. That fellow gets first crack at this matter. This just heightens the suspense a little more, winding it tighter. And, of course, you come to the end of the chapter in verse 18 and you're still on pins and needles because you don't know how the court situation is going to turn out. You have to wait until the next chapter to find out.

So there's a lot of suspense, isn't there?

Now, let's ask ourselves: why does Naomi resort to this kind of scheme? Well, because sometimes it's hard to move a man. It was also hard for them to get their concern across to Boaz. At that time, there were certain things that you didn't do.

For example, at the end of barley and wheat harvest, you don't put a post-it note on Boaz's thermos that reads, 'Boaz, we need to talk. My cell number is …, Love, Ruth.' You don't do that. That's just not the way you connect or get your point across. But neither was Naomi willing to just sit back and say, 'Sure was a fine barley harvest this year.' No, she wasn't willing to do that. She had her scheme worked out, and she wanted Ruth to carry it out.

So you have this daring plan by Naomi, who oddly seems to know exactly what Boaz was going to be doing that night. An interesting detail there.

Now, who is it who's acting this way? Think about Naomi for a minute. Well, she's a woman who believes that all things are in Yahweh's hands. Remember chapter 1, verses 13, 20, and 21? She says all these crushing things are in Yahweh's hands. You remember she said, 'The hand of Yahweh has gone out against me. The Almighty has deeply marred me. The Almighty has brought disaster on me.'

The crushing things are in God's hands. But then too, the caring things are in God's hands. Remember chapter 1, verses 8 and 9, where she wished a blessing upon Orpah and Ruth and said, 'May Yahweh deal kindly with you.' So there's a certain balance in Naomi's grief, and she knows that Yahweh does deal kindly with people and shows grace to them.

And at the same time, encouraging things are in his hands. Remember her reaction in chapter 2, verse 20, to that ephah of barley Ruth brought home? She said, 'May he [that is, Boaz] be blessed by Yahweh who has not forsaken his *hesed*, his kindness, to the living or the dead.'

So all these things are in Yahweh's hands. My point is that if you pushed Naomi, if you got down to brass tacks and said, 'Naomi, do you believe the Westminster Confession of Faith, chapter 5, section 1?', I think she would say yes. Well, you can find it in the back of your Trinity Hymnal, but let me remind you anyway: 'God, the great creator of all things, doth uphold, direct, dispose, and govern all creatures, actions, and things, from the greatest even to the least, by his most wise and holy providence.' I think that, from what Naomi says in the book of Ruth, she would agree with that.

God is absolutely sovereign, in charge of all matters. All right. And yet, though Naomi believes that, these women do not sit back and twiddle their thumbs. They take initiative.

I want you to see that. They do not see any conflict between divine providence and human ingenuity. They do not say: All is in God's hands; we can only sit back and wait. No, no. Do you see it? Believing in sovereign providence does not stifle but stimulates human action!

I'm not trying to explain that here. I just want you to observe it. Ephesians 1:11 speaks of 'God who works all things according to the counsel of his will.' But belief in a sovereign God who orders all things does not enervate you but energizes you to action. You see it in living color in Naomi.

It's the same mindset you hear from Stonewall Jackson after the Battle of First Manassas (or, Bull Run). Captain Imboden asked Jackson, 'General, how is it that you can keep so cool and appear to be utterly insensible to danger in such a storm of shells and bullets as you've just been through when your hand was wounded?'

Jackson replied, 'Captain, my religious belief teaches me to feel as safe in battle as in bed. God fixed a time for my death. I do not concern myself about that, but to be always ready no matter when it may overtake me. Captain, that is the way all men should live, and then all would be equally brave.'

Now don't get the wrong idea. Stonewall Jackson wasn't always right, but he was right there. And you know what he's saying. He's saying all things are in God's hands, and when you believe that, it doesn't freeze you with a Z. It frees you with an S. That's what he's saying, and he's absolutely right.

So if you believe that God works all things according to the counsel of his will, that sets you free to act. I can safely throw myself into whatever he calls me to do. You might say, 'But you don't know how it will turn out.' No, I don't know.

I don't control those things. God does, and that's what makes it so exciting.

God's sovereignty does not crush my activity. It invites it. However you explain it, it's right there in Ruth 3.

A Picture of God's Redemption

Secondly, we see here a picture of God's redemption. Look especially at verses 9 to 13. You have Ruth's request for marriage after she scares the daylights (I suppose) out of Boaz and he asks who she is.

She says, verse 9, 'I am Ruth, your handmaid – spread your wing over your handmaid, for you are a redeemer.' You are a *go'el* [go-ale] – that's the Hebrew term. You'll notice that throughout this part of the chapter, especially in verses 12 and 13, you have that root, translated 'redeem' or 'redeemer,' used about six times just in those two verses. But notice this request, 'Spread your wing.' It means the wing, as it were, of his cloak, the corner or edge of his cloak.

'Spread your wing over your maidservant.' It was a request for marriage. I don't have the time to go into the background of it. See Ezekiel 16, verse 8, for the picture. It's there. It was a request for marriage.

And of course you can see Boaz's reaction in verse 10. He's ecstatic. He's willing, and yet he's cautious because there is another relative who is in position, we could say, before Boaz. You see that in verse 12.

So Boaz was one of Naomi and Ruth's possible redeemers or benefactors in the family relationship. Remember, that was already mentioned in chapter 2, verse 20. But the fact is that there are others, including this man who is in line ahead of Boaz. Now Naomi and Ruth may have preferred

Boaz, and that might have been why they made this pitch (if one can call it that) to him. Something had to be done to get Boaz to consider the matter. And Boaz may have taken no initiative precisely because he knew there was another *go'el*, another relative, who was in position before he was, and so he backed away. That could be. In any case, he was not absolutely obligated to help or to marry Ruth or to help Naomi.

Now I know this is a big thing – and I don't want to get marooned in a bunch of details because we can lose ourselves in them, but this is not exactly a situation like you have in Deuteronomy 25, verses 5 to 10. There, you have a situation where you see a family, you have brothers living together, and one of them gets married. He dies, leaves no children, and so the law, the provision, is that the brother next after him is to marry the deceased brother's widow and raise up seed to that brother's name. But that's not exactly what's going on here in Ruth. There may of course be some connection, but it's not exactly the same.

Boaz is not a brother of Mahlon, Ruth's deceased husband. He's a family relative. Some of the principles in the latter half of Leviticus 25 may come into play here; but the Naomi-Ruth scenario is not exactly a textbook case.

At any rate, my only point here is that Boaz was not obligated to marry Ruth. This was not a 'have to' situation required by law. And so, this might have been why Naomi decided to go with this risky threshing floor scene, because it would be done, hopefully, in secret, and if Boaz refused to marry Ruth, no one else would know about it. Embarrassment would be minimal, both for Ruth and for Boaz. And...Ruth was not obligated to marry Boaz either.

That's what so overwhelmed Boaz in verse 10, because he essentially said, 'You know, you could have gotten any of the young bucks around town. You could have gotten one of those fellows who drink Gatorade outside the Circle K convenience store after work, or one of the younger merchants in the Bethlehem Rotary Club, but you didn't.' That implies that Boaz was a good deal older than Ruth. He is flattered; he may have been a decade or more older than Ruth. Ruth also was not obligated to seek out Boaz. That she did really impressed him.

'You could,' we can imagine him saying, 'have gotten any younger guy, but you didn't. You're still caring about other people. You're caring about Naomi and her care and provision, and so you want to marry in a family connection, and you want me to serve as redeemer, and take you under my care and protection – and Naomi as well.' And he's overwhelmed with that. Here's a woman who doesn't just follow her appetites or her selfish desires.

So we have, don't we, a kind of definition of what a redeemer, a *go'el*, is here in Ruth 3. A *go'el* or redeemer was a relative (verse 12) who protected (verse 9) the person and her rights, which in this case certainly involves ongoing provision and rescue from destitution. Or to put it more simply, a redeemer refers to a near relative who in our destitution takes us under his protection and provides for us. Now I want to touch on some implications of that, and I have two specifically in mind.

First, I think there's an implication here, an application, to Christian marriage. You notice in verse 9, Ruth says, 'Spread your wing, the wing of your garment, over your maidservant.' That was a request for marriage. But that implies a kind of protection in marriage, doesn't it? It's interesting that she uses that word 'wing' (literally).

That was a word that Boaz had used back in chapter 2, verse 12, when he commended Ruth because she had come under the protection of Yahweh's wings. That imagery is probably of a mother bird, the protection of a mother bird for her chicks. She had come under Yahweh's wings.

Now Ruth uses that same word, 'Spread your wing over me,' as if to say, perhaps, 'Boaz, why don't you answer in part your own prayer? You commended me to the care of Yahweh's wings – why don't you take me under your wing and give me a sample of that protectiveness?' And that, I think, is part of what Christian marriage should be. Isn't that implied in Ephesians 5, verses 25 and 29? 'Husbands, love your wives as Christ loved the church and gave himself up for her. For no one ever hated his own flesh but nourishes and cherishes it, just as Christ does the church.'

Ephesians 5:29 speaks of the protectiveness of Christian marriage. Of course, you may be one of those women who doesn't care about that. If you're one of those women who is so happy about being a 'strong' woman and you're proud of your biceps and you dismiss all this as too 'patriarchal'.... I'm sorry, I'm not talking to you.

But what you see here is that Christian marriage should be a protection for the woman. And sadly, sadly, even among Christians, this may not be the case. Oh, we're used to hearing of professional athletes, big hulks of fellows who smash other fellows on the football field – and also beat up their wives or their girlfriends. They're real tough. They can smash up girls. But sadly there are scores of so-called Christian husbands who verbally and physically abuse their wives. And it must be an ongoing, unending horror of fear and terror for those wives. And many of them are afraid to tell anyone. But some of the stories do come out.

And some of them, some of them, are ministers' wives. But in the marriage model of Christ and the church, the Christian husband stands in the position of the Lord Jesus Christ. And he should play the role of 'redeemer' to his wife. The husband should be the one who is near, to protect and provide.

Now, there's also, I think, a second implication of this picture of marriage here. In this picture in Ruth 3 you have a foregleam of the work of Jesus, our redeemer.

Isn't this the way Jesus functions toward us? He is the near relative who comes to our aid and delivers in our dire need, placing us under his protection and granting us his ongoing provision. Isn't that the capacity in which Jesus serves as our redeemer?

Now, you may think: where do you get that stuff about the near relative? Is Jesus our kinsman? Is he our relative? That's what the New Testament says. Isn't that the glory of that little word 'brother' in Romans 8:29, that Christ is the 'firstborn among many brothers'? Isn't that what's behind Hebrews 2:11 in that marvelous clause where it says, 'He is not ashamed to call them brothers'? And in verse 17 of the same chapter it says that 'he had to be made like his brothers in every respect.' Jesus is our near relative, our elder brother.

And the comfort that flows from that is immense. Martyn Lloyd-Jones told the story of a Covenanter girl back in about the 1680s, in Scotland. In those days she was going to attend a communion service that the Covenanters were holding on a Sunday afternoon. Of course, such services were strictly prohibited. The soldiers of the King of England were everywhere, seeking to apprehend people who were planning to go to this service.

She went to go to that service and came around a corner, coming smack dab, right face to face with a group of the King's soldiers. She knew she was trapped. For a moment, she wondered what she was going to say. But when they inquired of her, questioned her, she found herself answering: 'My elder brother has died,' and went on: 'They're going to read his will this afternoon. And he has done something for me, and he has left something for me, and I want to hear them read the will.' And they allowed her to go on.

As Lloyd-Jones said: 'Oh yes, her elder brother had died. Christ had died for her, and in the communion service, the will was going to be read out again. And she was going to be reminded of what he had done for her and what he had left for her.'

Now when you have a redeemer who is bound to you by family ties, like Jesus, our elder brother, you have all his provisions and resources as well. How then can we be poverty-stricken? No more than Ruth could ever be poverty-stricken after she was married to Boaz – a picture of Jesus as our redeemer.

A Sign of God's Mercies

Now thirdly, I want to point out one other matter that we see here, and that is a sign of God's mercies. In verses 15 to 18, you see how eager God is to give his servants snatches of assurance.

Here Boaz says to Ruth, very early in the morning before it was quite light, 'Bring the wrap you have, hold it out.' And he deposits six measures of barley into it. He then said, verse 17: 'You must not go empty to your mother-in-law.'

Now this is the third time in Ruth that a chapter ends with barley. You remember chapter one, verse 22 – they came to Bethlehem at the beginning of barley harvest. And that was important. That wasn't just a chronological marker because there had been a famine and this year there *was* a barley harvest.

And then in chapter 2, about verse 17, you recall that Ruth brought home an ephah of barley from her pickings and gleanings. That's about three-fifths of a bushel. And Naomi is impressed and she blesses Yahweh, 'who has not forsaken his *hesed*, his kindness, to the living or the dead.' She was ecstatic over that sign that God had not forgotten her.

Now at the end of chapter three, verse 17, you've got more barley. Ruth is the barley book of the Bible.

So what is the function of this? You notice that Boaz says, 'you must not go home empty to your mother-in-law.' That picks up a word that Naomi had used in chapter one, verse 21: 'I went away full, and Yahweh has brought me back empty.' And now Boaz picks up that word: 'you mustn't go back to your mother-in-law empty.' As if to say, perhaps, 'You mustn't let Naomi think she's running on empty. She needs to know that the Lord is still providing for her even in small ways.'

Now you might say, well, you made a similar point like that at the end of the exposition of Ruth, chapter two. Yes, I did. So why repeat it here? Because it's in the text. It's there. It comes up again, and it may seem to you like a small matter. It's only a few measures of barley and most of you probably wouldn't care whether you had a few measures of barley or not. But for Naomi, it would matter a lot. What may seem insignificant to us can be very telling to others, because small signs leave big impressions on needy people.

Sometimes we can pass small things like this off as insignificant, can't we? That's sort of like the way I suppose Americans viewed the movie, 'The Grapes of Wrath.' I never saw the movie. I read the book. But *The Grapes of Wrath* by John Steinbeck was made into a movie. And if you've seen it, you remember how it depicted the downside of American life back in 'depression' days and how miserable things were and so on.

But, wouldn't you know, Joe Stalin wouldn't allow that movie to be shown in the Soviet Union. You might wonder, 'Why not?' After all, it makes Americans and the United States look like they are at the end of their tether. It's really dire and sad and miserable.

But Joe Stalin said something like this: 'Yes, well, but it shows that people have trucks and they can go anywhere they want.'

Trucks? That rickety piece of junk they had in the movie? You think that's absurd, but some people, like Stalin, saw that as significant. It was too 'political' for Joe to let his people see that some poor folks had mobility and could go where they wanted.

We wouldn't think much of it, but it was telling to Stalin. And here, this gift of barley is just another indication, a small assurance to Naomi that the Lord has not forgotten her. Now there may be some small token the Lord has given you and you are not seeing it. Maybe there's some low-key way in which God has reminded you that you aren't running on empty. And you owe him thanks for that. I mean, such tokens don't solve your troubles. They don't replace your losses. They don't dissolve your heartaches. These little signs don't eliminate your tragedies and they don't wipe out your sorrow, but they simply say, like a few measures of barley, 'Even in this, I have not forgotten you.'

Sometimes that's all you need in the moment. You might think that's not much. You're right, but it may be just the sign of God's mercies that gets you through Tuesday.

So in one sense nothing is settled. Look at verse 18: you're hanging over the edge of a literary cliff. You don't know how it's going to turn out. But, with Naomi, we can trust a willing redeemer to handle all the affairs that concern us.

4 A GOOD DAY IN COURT
(Ruth 4:1-12)

(1) Now Boaz went up to the gate and sat there, and there was the redeemer passing by whom Boaz had spoken of! So he said, 'Turn aside, sit here, what's your name.' So he turned aside and sat down.

(2) And he got ten men from the town's elders and said, 'Sit here,' and they sat down.

(3) Then he said to the redeemer, 'The portion of the field which belonged to our brother Elimelech – Naomi who returned from the territory of Moab is selling it.

(4) And I thought I would let you know, saying, "Acquire it in the presence of those sitting here, especially in the presence of the elders of my people"; if you want to redeem it, redeem it, and if you will not redeem it, tell me that I may know, for there's no one besides you to redeem it, and I come after you.' And he said, 'I want to redeem it.'

(5) Then Boaz said, 'On the day of your acquiring the field from Naomi, you acquire Ruth the Moabitess, the wife of the dead, to raise up the name of the dead upon his inheritance.'

(6) And the redeemer said, 'I will not be able to redeem it for myself, lest I ruin my inheritance; you take on yourself my right of redemption, for I cannot redeem it.'

(7) Now this is the way it used to be in Israel in matters of redemption and exchanging to confirm every matter: a man pulled off his sandal and gave it to his counterpart. And this was the way of attesting something in Israel.

(8) So the redeemer said to Boaz, 'Acquire it for yourself,' then he pulled off his sandal.

(9) And Boaz said to the elders and all the people, 'You are witnesses today, that I have acquired all that belonged to Elimelech and all that belonged to Chilion and Mahlon from the hand of Naomi,

(10) and what's more, Ruth the Moabitess, the wife of Mahlon, I've acquired for my wife to raise up a name for the dead upon his inheritance, that the name of the dead may not be cut off from among his brothers and from the gate of his place. You are witnesses today.'

(11) And all the people who were in the gate, along with the elders, said, 'We are witnesses. May Yahweh grant that the woman who is coming into your house may be like Rachel and like Leah, who both built up the house of Israel, that you may accomplish much in Ephrathah and be famous in Bethlehem,

(12) that your household might be like the household of Perez, whom Tamar bore to Judah, from the seed which Yahweh will give to you from this girl.'

You always learn something from serving on jury duty, even if it always comes at an inconvenient time. Once while we were living in Baltimore, I was called up for jury duty. It was 1989, and they were trying to conjure up a jury for some sort of civil injury case for something that had taken place four to five years before.

It was such a backlog, such a slow way of getting around to matters, it seemed; but things were much more efficient in Bethlehem. You can see from the form of the court case there in your text that it consisted of calling the parties and the witnesses together, as in verses 1 and 2. You notice that when Boaz sees this redeemer, who's a nearer relative than Boaz is to Naomi's family, Boaz summons him and in the Hebrew calls him *peloni 'almoni* (long o's). It sounds like an Italian immigrant to Bethlehem! Scholars don't know what that means exactly. It was apparently an expression that was meant to refer to him without actually using his name. Maybe something like our 'Joe Schmo.'

It might be that the writer edited Boaz's comment so that it didn't reveal the actual name of the fellow who was involved here. We don't know. But *peloni 'almoni* sits down, and then there's the presentation of the case in verses 3 and the first part of verse 4. And then in the last of verse 4 through 6, Boaz prosecutes the matter to a decision, and gets a decision from the fellow. Then there's the matter of attesting things. First of all, verses 7 and 8, between the two parties, and then attesting it by witnesses that actually observed the exchange in verses 9 to the first part of verse 11. After that, there's the blessing of the court. Maybe you wouldn't have that where you live, but, in Bethlehem, the court prays for you.

Now, we've been in suspense since chapter 3, verse 18. How will the matter fall out after the episode at the threshing floor? How will everything be resolved? Well, it will fall out in court, which takes place in an eastern town, in the city gate, which had places for gathering and assembly.

And so we come to the fourth major scene of the Book of Ruth. You may remember that we called the dominant scene in chapter 1 'on the road.' In chapter 2, it was 'in the field.' In chapter 3, it was 'at the threshing floor.' And now in chapter 4, verses 1 to 12, the scene is 'before the court.' That's where we are.

And by this point, we can say that sometimes, sometimes, the people God afflicts begin to see the goodness of the Lord in the land of the living. So, in our rather pedantic way of facing these texts, I simply want to ask, What are we meant to see or to hear from this passage?

The Costly Commitment of God's Redeemer

First, we are going to look at the costly commitment of God's redeemer, taking a big glob of the text, verses 1 to 10. Now you have the situation presented there in verses 3 and 4. 'The portion of the field,' Boaz said, 'which belonged to our brother Elimelech – Naomi, who returned from the territory of Moab, is selling it. And I thought I would let you know, saying, "Acquire it in the presence of those sitting here,"' – and so on. Then Boaz says, 'If you'll redeem it, all right. If not, let me know. I come after you.'

So there's the situation. Now, we don't have all the info that we would like to have. In fact, this is the first we know anything of any portion of a field that Naomi might be selling. And that's perfectly all right. Scholars get bent out of shape because we didn't know anything about this before. You can read pages and pages about this, and you'll find views and views. But maybe the writer just thought, 'Well, why should I tell them before now? I can let Boaz tell them in court.' And so we find out about it now.

Let me just give you a couple of scenarios about what may be reflected here in verses 3 and 4, as best as we can put things together.

One scenario might be that Naomi seems to have had rights to her husband Elimelech's property. Although she can't sell that land permanently, she could sell the use of the land. It would be sold in terms of the number of years that one could get a crop from it before it would go back to her. You can see some of this background in Leviticus 25. And so maybe Naomi is now selling the use of the land in order to sustain herself because she's in poverty, and Boaz wants himself or this other fellow among her relatives to buy the use of the land from her so that the land stays in the family.

Or it could be that Elimelech sold the use of the land before he took his family to Moab. So when it says here that Naomi is 'selling,' it means that Naomi is asking someone in the family connection, like Boaz or this other fellow, to buy back the use of the land so the family can use it again.

In any case, the nearer relative smells real estate, and he says (last of verse 4), 'I will redeem it.' Then Boaz throws a curveball in verse 5, although there's nothing really devious about it. He's just smart in the way he puts the case, that's all.

So Boaz says, 'On the day of your acquiring' (and please understand, I realize that there are big issues about how one should translate this verse; I'm trying not to go into all that – we would just lose ourselves), 'On the day of your acquiring the field from Naomi, you acquire Ruth the Moabitess, the wife of the dead, to raise up the name of the dead upon his inheritance.'

There's a package deal here, Boaz says. Now, it's kind of hard to put all the pieces together to figure out just what's involved in this. Here's the best that I can do. You remember when we dealt with chapter 3 (if you don't, that's all right).

I tried to make the point there in chapter 3 that Ruth is not obligated to marry Boaz. Boaz himself says she could have married anyone. Anyone. The field was open for her. She could have gone after anyone she wanted. And also, Boaz was not obligated to marry Ruth, even when she asked him to marry her and take her under his protection. But Boaz decided he was willing to marry her. He chose to. There was no 'have to' in either case.

And yet, here in chapter 4, there seems to be this provision that in this case, that if you seek to redeem the land, to buy back the use of the land from Naomi, there's more involved. It involves marrying Ruth. It involves raising up a descendant by Mahlon's widow. Now, as I said, this was not an absolute obligation on Boaz's part. But if he willingly assumes it, as he said he would do in chapter 3, verse 11, then he would go ahead with it too.

Some people think this is levirate marriage or brother-in-law marriage. You recall we talked about that a little, referencing Deuteronomy 25. There's that setup, that law that says that if you have brothers, if they are all dwelling in the same household, and one of them marries a wife and he dies, then the next brother in line is to marry her. Her brother-in-law marries her and is to raise up a child to his brother's name. And that was almost a requirement. The fellow could get out of it with a great deal of shame, but it was basically a requirement.

But there's not that kind of requirement here. Boaz isn't a brother of Mahlon. There is a voluntary element here. And yet what seems to be the case is that you have something like the law of Deuteronomy 25 in the background, but it's kind of loosened up a bit. And perhaps over the years some customs have arisen which were based on the original law, but which didn't carry the same compulsion to marry the widow if the relatives are more distant. So it's sort of like Deuteronomy 25, but it doesn't have the same expectation or pressure behind it.

Now, this fellow then, when he realizes what it all involves, says, 'Whoa, can't do it. Sorry. It would ruin my inheritance.' We don't need to go into what all that might involve, but he backs out.

And as one writer says, if it just involved the use of the land and redeeming the land back, this fellow could perform a respected family duty. He could enhance his reputation for having done so. He could gain land that on Naomi's death would then become his.

But as another writer points out, with Boaz's twist – that is, if you redeem the land, you also have to marry Ruth and raise up a child – now he would have to support two women, and pay for the field, and there would be another mouth to feed if Ruth gave birth to a child, and then that child would inherit the land.

So either he couldn't or he wouldn't. In any case, he backs out. It's not as attractive a bargain as he thought it would be.

Things are like that sometimes. They're not as attractive once we look at them a little closer. Sort of like the time when Mary, Queen of Scots, was executed under the reign of Elizabeth I. The executioner did a poor job. It took him two and a half whacks to get the job done. And when he held up Mary's head and said, 'God save the queen,' he was holding a pile of auburn curls and a little white cap, because her head had dropped out and rolled like a misshapen football toward the spectators. She had been wearing a wig, and the people noticed that her head was actually very gray and nearly bald.

Mary, the charming, vivacious, attractive Queen of Scots. She was only 44 years old when executed, but she had a wig. And when folks saw what she really looked like, she wasn't nearly as attractive as they at first thought. That may seem a bit too gory for you, but that's the way it is here in the text. This fellow says the situation isn't very attractive to him once he knows what the package deal is. And so he backs out.

Notice then the commitment made by Boaz in verses 9 and 10. He calls on the court to bear witness that he's acquired all that belonged to Elimelech, et cetera.

In verse 10, the words 'Ruth the Moabitess, the wife of Mahlon' are in emphatic position in the Hebrew text. It's as if Boaz knows what he's really interested in and who really has his heart! 'Ruth the Moabitess, the wife of Mahlon, I've acquired for my wife, to raise up a name for the dead.' So here you have the commitment that Boaz makes. And it's a costly obligation. The other fellow backed out because of the costliness involved. Boaz willingly takes it up. He will suffer material loss if need be.

Some Old Testament laws were like that. They didn't necessarily reward the person who obeyed them. They might deplete him. For instance, in Exodus 34, the law about keeping the sabbath. You work six days, you rest the seventh day, even in plowing time and harvest. You might say, 'But it's going to rain!' That's all right. Just let it rain. Maybe you'll have better success with crops next year. But you suffer a loss if need be.

And here, Boaz is willing to commit himself to what you might call a losing proposition financially. He's sticking with the costly way. He's as good as his word in chapter 3, verse 11.

Now this, of course, brings up a sort of a foreshadowing, doesn't it? I don't mean that there's any direct prophecy here, but there's a kind of marvelous picture here, isn't there, of the Lord Jesus Christ's commitment to us as his people, about the way he will give himself for us? You remember the contrast Jesus drew between himself and the hired hand in John 10.

The hired hand sees the wolf coming, and he leaves the sheep and flees, because he's a hired hand, and he doesn't really care about the sheep. The sheep don't belong to him, and, when push comes to shove, he doesn't give a rip about them. By contrast Jesus claims, 'I am the good shepherd.' The good shepherd lays down his life for the sheep, defends them to the end, gives himself to death if need be. He's not a hired hand.

That's the commitment Jesus makes to his people. It's the commitment reflected in Romans 15, where it says Christ did not please himself. It's the commitment reflected in Jesus' words in John 6:38, when he says, 'I've come down from heaven, not to do my own will, but the will of him who sent me.'

It's the commitment prophesied of him in Isaiah 53:12, when it says he poured out his soul to death. That's what he does for his people. That's the costly commitment.

It's the commitment of Philippians 2:6-7, where it says that Christ, existing in the form of God, did not consider equality with God as something to be used for his own advantage. Instead, he emptied himself by assuming the form of a slave.

You might say it's a losing proposition. It's a costly one, and he commits himself to it because of his commitment to his people. And doesn't that explain, in part, our love for him?

Os Guinness tells the story of one of the periodic efforts in the Soviet Union to eradicate religious belief. The Communist Party sent out KGB agents to various churches across the nation on a certain Sunday morning.

One agent was struck by the deep devotion of an elderly woman who was kissing the feet of a life-sized carving of Christ on the cross. And so he said to her, 'Babushka [grandmother], are you also prepared to kiss the feet of the beloved General Secretary of our great Communist Party?' 'Why, of course,' she shot back, 'but only if you crucify him first.' That's it – there is something about the costly commitment of our Redeemer that wins and explains our love for him.

And you see a faint depiction of that in the commitment of Boaz. Jesus had a Boaz complex about him.

The Expectant Prayer of God's People

Secondly, we're meant to see (or hear) here the expectant prayer of God's people, in verses 11 and 12.

You don't usually leave court with a prayer blessing ringing in your ears, but you did in Bethlehem. You'll notice that there's a particular prayer here in verse 11. The people and the elders said, 'We are witnesses,' and then they go on to announce this blessing prayer:

> May Yahweh grant that the woman who is coming
> into your house may be like Rachel and like Leah,
> who both built up the house of Israel.

One thing that this prayer asks for is productivity, to put it bluntly. They're praying, as they say in verse 12, for 'the seed which Yahweh will give to you from this girl.' They're praying for babies, and you notice that they allude to Rachel and Leah, Jacob's main wives, who built up the house of Israel along with their maidservants. You can read all about that in Genesis 29 and 30. It was sort of like a soap opera in an OB ward, but at the end of it all, there were those kids. God had been faithful to his promise.

There's also a prayer for prominence. You note that in verse 12: 'May your household be like the household of Perez, whom Tamar bore to Judah.' There you are going back to Genesis 38, that twisted narrative in which Tamar finally gives birth to Perez by her father-in-law Judah. But Perez was the head of one of the main clans of the tribe of Judah – in fact, the clan of which Boaz was a part. So they're asking for a certain prominence to be given to Boaz and the child from this marriage.

Now this prayer is needed here because the suspense at this point is even higher than at the threshing floor and at the town gate. We don't know how many years of marriage Ruth and Mahlon had in Moab. Six years? Eight years? We don't know, but we do know there had never been a child. During her marriage, Ruth had been barren.

She has never had a child. So you get past the crisis of the threshing floor: Will Boaz be willing to 'cover' Ruth in marriage? Well, yes, he is. That suspense is out of the way. But then there's a nearer redeemer, a nearer relative. What will happen if he wants to perform the right of redemption? Well, the court scene takes care of that, so that's solved. But we're still not home free. What if this marriage doesn't produce an heir? Because, so far, Ruth hasn't had or been able to have a child.

And so, if you're thinking in terms of literary suspense, you're on the edge of a literary cliff almost to the very end. Only verse 13 will relieve that suspense. But what I want you to see here is that this prayer is not just a neat little ditty that's unnecessary. On the contrary, it addresses a real need.

I think this also leads us to think in terms of the general view of prayer we see in the book of Ruth. There are an awful lot of prayers in the book of Ruth for such a short book, and they are prayers for blessing.

As someone has said, all the prayers in the book of Ruth are answered, but not necessarily in the way that could be foreseen. For example, in chapter one, verses eight and nine, Naomi utters that blessing upon Ruth and Orpah: 'May Yahweh deal kindly (or show *hesed*-love, his faithful love) to you as you have done with the dead and with me. May you find rest in the house of your husband,' that is, in the house of another husband. Now we don't know what happened to Orpah, but for Ruth, Naomi's prayer is answered in Ruth's marriage to Boaz.

And then, of course, you have the prayer in chapter two, verse 12, where Boaz says to Ruth, 'May Yahweh give you a full reward, Yahweh, under whose wings you have come to take refuge.' And oddly enough, that prayer was answered as well (with a little persuasion from Ruth at the threshing floor) in chapter 3. You recall how Ruth picked up Boaz's reference to Yahweh's wings when she said: 'Now take me under your wings; spread your wing over me in marriage and give me that protection.' It's as if she's saying: Why don't you yourself, Boaz, help to answer your own prayer? And he was willing to do so.

Then you have this prayer in chapter four, verses 11 to 12. You'll see it begin to be answered in verse 13. We don't know that it's answered with twelve children, but it's answered with at least one child that we know of.

So these prayers for blessing are answered.

What are we to make of this? I think on reflection we should say we should not take prayer lightly. These prayers for blessing in this book are not just neat little ditties. Yahweh takes them quite seriously, obviously. And that's not surprising, perhaps, because Psalm 65 addresses Yahweh as 'the one who hears prayer.' And, indeed, he does. Since Yahweh seems to esteem his people's prayers so much, then we should esteem prayer too. And therefore we should also take great care with our prayers as well.

I was struck reading one of the anecdotes of Rabbi Duncan. He was a very godly but very eccentric Old Testament professor in Scotland around the 1840s or so. The Lord made John Duncan and then threw away the mold. There was no one quite like him. He was a bit strange, and he was always wrestling with assurance of salvation and that sort of thing. But one time, one of his friends and maybe a former student, Moody Stuart, asked Dr Duncan, or Rabbi Duncan as he was known, if he would come to his congregation and preach for him – fill the pulpit for him.

And Rabbi Duncan said, 'I'll be glad to preach if you take the prayers. I'm not able to pray at present, but I can preach a bit. I would like it. I'll be glad to preach if you take the prayers.' Now that doesn't mean preaching is easy. It comes with a bit of distress and anguish all the time. But really, anyone can preach – if you just do the work. But prayer, that's something more. 'I'll be glad to preach if you take the prayers.'

We need to esteem the whole matter of prayer because Yahweh our God esteems the prayers of his people. The Book of Ruth tells us that that is so.

The Strange Quirks of God's Program

And then I think we ought to notice, thirdly, the strange quirks of God's program.

Did you catch that name at the end of their prayer? We're looking at verse 12 here, when they said, 'We want your household to be like the household of Perez whom Tamar bore to Judah.'

Tamar – you can find her in Genesis 38, if you don't remember. The tribal ancestor Judah fathered twins by Tamar, one of whom was mentioned in our text. He's the head of one of the tribe's major clans.

Tamar was apparently a Canaanite. And her scheme in Genesis 38 made Naomi's threshing floor plan look like kindergarten play, believe me. I can't prove it, but I wonder if the very presence of Ruth didn't bring Tamar to mind for these folks at the city gate.

You see, all through the book of Ruth, six times Ruth is called 'Ruth the Moabitess' or 'Ruth the Moabite girl' – however your version translates it. She's always the Moabitess. She's the outsider. She's the foreigner. She's the one who isn't a part of Israel.

Perhaps when these folks think of Ruth, they think back to Tamar. Yes, there was Tamar, apparently a Canaanite, who wasn't within the family of Jacob either. God used Tamar, and now again he's using this Moabite girl. And Yahweh seems to be bringing her among us and using her to build up our tribal family.

God seems to have two ways of doing things, doesn't he? The ordinary and the unconventional. And you have the Tamars and the Ruths who are made a part of God's plan in bringing redemption into his world. And it breaks the mold that we sometimes create for him.

There's something utterly refreshing, isn't there, about God's unconventionality? I find it refreshing to see that trait in people sometimes. Sometimes it is just plain weirdness. But sometimes people have a certain unconventionality that's rather attractive and endearing.

I think I found it in my father. I have some of my father's pastoral reports that he used to give to his congregation. Normally these were one-page type-written reports, and they would cover a year of his pastoral ministry among a certain congregation. It would cover, say 1935, and the report might be given in January of 1936 at the 'congregational meeting.' He would read his report to the people.

In 1935 he was serving a three-church charge. He preached, I think, every Sunday at all three churches, and maybe even had an evening service at one of them. So he was very busy. In addition, they had prayer meetings in two of the congregations sometime during the week.

And he said in his report there were 36 prayer meetings conducted at the one church, and 23 prayer meetings conducted at another. He also reported what was covered in the Bible study portion of the prayer meetings. Then he made this comment at the end of a paragraph: 'The greater part of both these congregations [which I will refer to as *peloni 'almoni* since I don't want to name them here] apparently do not value the prayer meetings as they never attend.' That's in his report and he read that to the congregations.

Surely he was not that blunt. No, but he was. But they might be offended. Well, maybe they needed to be offended. It just breaks the mold of the usual churchy nicety.

Sometimes pastors are asked to candidate at another congregation, possibly to receive a 'call' to that church. So in his pastoral report to the congregation he was serving in 1956, he actually said this: 'Two opportunities to candidate were received during the year from Pitcairn, Pennsylvania and from Harrisville and Uniontown, Ohio. Family conditions dictated that these invitations be refused, although they offered nice increases in salary.'

Who has the gall to say something like that? But there's something refreshing about such candor – perilous as it might be. Unconventional. And that's the way, oftentimes, the God of the Bible is.

God is always faithful, but he's not always predictable. Sometimes he does outlandish things. He doesn't blush to use a Moabite girl as his handmaid in carrying out his kingdom plan.

Indeed, there's something very Tamar-ish and Ruth-ish about the fact of your own position because most of you are not Israelites after the flesh. Have you ever pondered Romans 11, verses 17-24? You remember when Paul compares the people of God, especially Israel, to an olive tree, and he's speaking to non-Israelite believers, and says:

> But if some of the branches were broken off and you, although a wild olive shoot, were grafted in among the others and now share in the nourishing root of the olive tree....

It's as if he's saying to Gentile believers, 'You didn't belong! But God took you as if you were a wild olive shoot and grafted you in!' It's hard for us, perhaps, to get into that mentality that was so pervasive in the New Testament period. But you didn't belong. You were on the outside. You had no place nor right to be among the people of God. But God gave you a place.

You were grafted in! You were alienated, as Paul says, from the commonwealth of Israel. You're a bunch of Tamar and Ruth clones, and you were brought near by the blood of the Messiah (Eph. 2:13). And what praise you owe, because Yahweh is miraculously unconventional, to wrap the arms of his covenant around you and graft you in so that you piggyback on Israel's blessings.

That's not too bad for a day in court. Think what it must have meant for Naomi to sense that sometimes the people whom God afflicts begin to see the goodness of the Lord in the land of the living.

5 NURSERY AND HISTORY
(Ruth 4:13-22)

(13) So Boaz took Ruth and she became his wife; and he went in to her, and Yahweh gave her conception, and she gave birth to a son.

(14) Then the women said to Naomi, 'Blessed be Yahweh, who has not allowed a redeemer to fail for you today – and may his name be famous in Israel!

(15) And he shall be for you one who restores life and one to sustain you in your old age, because your daughter-in-law who loves you has given birth to him – she's better to you than seven sons.'

(16) So Naomi took the child and placed him in her lap and took care of him.

(17) And the neighbor women named him, saying, 'A son has been born to Naomi.' And they named him Obed; he is the father of Jesse, the father of David.

(18) Now these are the developments that came from Perez:
Perez fathered Hezron,

(19) and Hezron fathered Ram,
and Ram fathered Amminadab,

(20) and Amminadab fathered Nahshon,
and Nahshon fathered Salmon,

(21) and Salmon fathered Boaz,
and Boaz fathered Obed,

(22) and Obed fathered Jesse,
and Jesse fathered David.

There was a fellow who came into a hospital in western France a few years ago. He had a very sore stomach, couldn't eat, couldn't move his bowels, really in bad shape. So they did an X-ray on him and saw a rather huge mass there in the X-ray. It turned out it weighed twelve pounds. It seems that it consisted of 350 coins that he had swallowed over a period of time. It's very hard to mix digestion and coins. They don't go together very well.

And, in a way, you might say, 'You know, this text doesn't go together very well.' On the one hand, you have a nice birth story here, and then you have what's apparently a dry as dust genealogy. They just don't go together. They don't mix well.

But we're going to keep them together anyway, because these two seemingly dissimilar sections are the final scene in the book. We've already touched on the other scenes. We said scene 1 is in chapter 1. We called it 'on the road.' Chapter 2 was 'in the barley field' or 'in the field.' And chapter 3 is 'at the threshing floor.' Chapter 4, verses 1 to 12, was 'before the court.' Now here in chapter 4, verses 13 to 22, we are 'beyond the nursery.' This scene begins in the nursery, but it doesn't stay there. So it's 'beyond the nursery.'

The main truth of this section of text – indeed, you could probably say the main truth of the whole Book of Ruth – is just this: *God takes the common and complicated circumstances in the lives of his people and makes them contribute to the coming of his kingdom in this world.*

How ought we to come at the teaching of the text? I think we'll try to sum it up in several propositions about faith.

Faith must not lose sight of the necessity of divine blessing

The first proposition is just this: faith must not lose sight of the necessity of divine blessing. And that's in verse 13: 'So Boaz took Ruth and she became his wife; and he went in to her, and Yahweh gave her conception and she gave birth to a son.'

The text here, verse 13, is one of two texts in the book that speaks of a direct divine intervention. One of them is in chapter 1, verse 6, where it says, 'Naomi heard that Yahweh had looked after his people by giving them food.' And so the famine was over. And then here, in chapter 4, verse 13, 'Yahweh gave her conception.' Only two texts in the whole book directly speak of divine intervention and specifically tell us what Yahweh was up to! And these are very basic matters in both texts – 1:6 is food and 4:13 is fertility. Pretty basic stuff.

Now the Hebrews knew the facts of life. They also knew, though, that life was more than sperm and egg and zygote. They knew that life was a gift from Yahweh. And that's what the text is telling us. Yahweh gave her conception. Life is his gift. It's not merely the result of two people who 'know how to do it.'

What you notice, however, is that most of the narrative in the book of Ruth is not like this. The pattern in the book overall is not to speak directly about what Yahweh is doing. It doesn't stop along the way and say, 'No, Yahweh did that, no, God did that,' and so on. That would ruin the story for you in a way. You don't want to hear that all the time, I suppose. So the writer simply describes the ordinary run of things, doesn't he? And he expects you to see God at work in these things. For example, Ruth's decision to cling to Naomi and to Naomi's God. Or how the writer just expects you to divine what he means when he wrote in chapter 2 that Ruth 'just happened' to come into the portion of the field belonging to Boaz. Or how he expects you to see Yahweh working behind Naomi's threshing floor scheme and behind Boaz's decision to gladly do what Ruth asked him to do, and behind the first redeemer's refusal to exercise his rights, leaving the field open for Boaz. The writer expects you to be able to do that through the normal description of the story.

Yahweh is working, even though it seems very low-key. That's the beauty of the narrative, isn't it? We don't want a writer doing frequent stops and saying, 'Now it was really Yahweh who did this.' It's the seeming ordinariness of Yahweh's ways that is so enjoyable.

It's the indirectness of the story that we love. Now, if you're thirty-five years of age or younger, you may not get this, so you can tune out if you want ....

It's sort of like a fellow and a gal in college, and let's say they're dating, or at least they go out on different occasions, and so on. And the guy comes to a place where he thinks, 'You know, I'd really like to hold hands with her.'

But then he thinks, 'That's a touchy thing, in more ways than one. Because if I try that, she might get scared off. And this one's too good a deal to scare away. So what am I going to do?' So if you're that fellow, you're in a kind of anguish about holding her hand. She doesn't seem uninterested though. I mean, every time you ask her out to go, maybe to a college event or something, she always says yes. And so that's encouraging. But you don't want to press your luck.

And you can imagine that if the girl was thinking about the same matter, she might say to herself, 'Oh my, I can't take any initiative here; he'd think I'm too aggressive.' So you see there can be some real angst and turmoil over wanting to hold hands.

Now there's just one thing you don't do in a situation like that. You don't become direct. You don't say, 'Now look, we really need to have a talk about this matter of holding hands. We need to make a decision about this, set a date when it might begin. We need to just hit this head on.' Oh, man, that would wreck the whole thing. That's just plain crud. It's the anguish and uncertainty that is the fun of it all.

That makes it so interesting and keeps you tied in knots. And you wouldn't trade it for the world. And you don't have to, because indirectness so often works, doesn't it? It just takes care of itself.

So you're walking down the main sidewalk through the middle of campus one evening. And as you both walk along, it just happens that your hands happen to brush one another a little bit and they clasp, and it's all over. But it's so beautiful that way. It simply happens! You don't have to make some explicit decision, do you? That's the beauty of it, this indirectness. And that's the way most of the narrative in Ruth reads.

But then chapter 4, verse 13, is direct. It's explicit. Why is that? Why does it say Yahweh gave her conception? What's the point? The point is to teach the necessity of divine blessing (and not merely leave it to your inferences).

You may recall Psalm 127: 'Unless Yahweh builds the house, the builders toil in vain. Unless Yahweh watches over the city, the watchman stays awake in vain.' That watchman can shoot caffeine directly into his veins, but it won't do any good unless Yahweh guards the city. There has to be more than human effort.

Unless the Lord builds the house, the builders labor in vain. It's God's doing that must be behind human effort and it's his blessing that is so needed. And here, everything in the whole story is zilch if Ruth remains childless. And so it's important that the writer underscores that the child is a gift. Yahweh's gift. Yahweh gave her conception. Sometimes you have to say it directly, because sometimes faith can lose sight of the necessity of divine blessing.

Cornelius Ryan tells of a time in 1945 when the Red Army troops came into Berlin and were capturing part of it. You have to understand that some of these Soviet troops were probably from country areas and had not been exposed to an advanced city like Berlin. Ryan says that they actually would unscrew light bulbs and carefully pack them away, because they thought that they contained light and would work anywhere. You would have said to them, 'Oh, no, no, it can't be that way. Why, you have to have electricity and a lamp and infrastructure' and so on. But no, those Soviet soldiers just saw the light bulbs and thought, 'Those will work anywhere. Let's take them with us.'

You always have to see what's behind things. You have to see the divine blessing behind the gift. And that's what you have in this Ruth story. Sometimes the Bible wants to explicitly underscore that. Sometimes the Bible wants you to see things don't happen automatically or as a matter of course.

We tend to think we have rights. That we're entitled to stuff. But the text is saying, 'No, you mustn't forget that everything is of grace. Everything is gift. You can make the fullest human efforts you want, but you must still have divine blessing. In this particular case, it has to do with Ruth's conception. Yahweh gave her conception. That was a gift.

But this isn't true in only Ruth's particular matter. There's a sense in which this is the case promiscuously across the board in God's dealing with us. We need to remember that as well.

Martin Luther did a delightful piece of work in his small catechism. And sometimes the churches we served would use segments of it as a confession of faith in worship. Now, it's written from the standpoint of a male householder – if you find that 'offensive,' then skip this. But it's a delightful piece. He begins by taking up the first article of the Apostles' Creed, 'I believe in God the Father Almighty, maker of heaven and earth.' What does this mean?, he asks. Here is Luther's answer:

> I believe that God has created me and all that exists, that he has given and still preserves to me body and soul, eyes, ears, and all my limbs, my reason, and all my senses, and also clothing and shoes, food and drink, house and home, wife and child, land, cattle, and all my property, that he provides me richly and daily with all the necessaries of life, protects me from all danger, and preserves and guards me against all evil, and all this out of pure paternal divine goodness and mercy without any merit or worthiness of mine, for all of which I am in duty bound to thank, praise, serve, and obey him. This is most certainly true.

That's Luther. Now, I don't know for sure, because I'm not an expert on confessions and credal statements, but this is the only one I know of that mentions shoes. I love that. It's so earthy, isn't it?

In Ruth 4:13 the writer has good reason to make the point that Yahweh is behind Ruth's conception. But you also need to look at the broad scope, at the whole run of all our matters and all our affairs, and remember that the divine blessing is there as well.

It's all God's gift. How many times have you thanked the Lord for your reason or your shoes? That's why Isaac Watts reminds us in the hymn (based on Psalm 103):

> O bless the Lord, my soul,
> nor let his mercies lie
> forgotten in unthankfulness
> and without praises die.

Faith must not lose sight of the necessity of divine blessing.

Faith can scarcely grasp the intensity of God's care

Here's a second proposition: Faith can scarcely grasp the intensity of God's care.

Let's examine verses 14 to 17 here in the light of everything that's happened so far in the Book of Ruth. Look at what the women tell Naomi in verses 14 and 15.

First, they tell Naomi what she has. 'Blessed be Yahweh,' verse 14, 'who has not allowed a redeemer to fail for you today.' You've got a redeemer. They're talking about Obed, this baby in the nursery that she's holding. That's what she has.

And then they tell Naomi what she will have in the first part of verse 15: 'And he shall be for you one who restores life and one to sustain you in your old age.' He's going to take care of you in the future.

And they tell Naomi what she has had in the last of verse 15: 'Because your daughter-in-law who loves you has given birth to him – she's better to you than seven sons.' Verses 14 and 15 don't sound like Naomi is 'empty,' like she said she was in chapter 1. Rather, she sounds pretty 'full.'

Now let's look at verses 14 to 17 in the sense that these verses are part of a pattern. Let's put them in the context of the whole book and see what they show us. When we do this, although it's almost beyond us to imagine, we see how intensely our Father cares for his bruised and broken people.

Naomi may not have seen what I'm going to explain to you here. She may not have seen it in her experiences; but, you see, we have a book. We have a literary document that has a certain scheme to it and makes certain points and wants to underscore certain things for us.

So, although we're not experiencing it like Naomi did, we're reading it. So what is the point in the reading of this story that the Lord is trying to bring home to us? I want you to notice how every chapter returns our attention to Naomi.

Now of course, in chapter one, having our attention on Naomi is very natural. You say, 'Obviously, for the narrative has been focused on Naomi and Ruth and Orpah, and on Naomi and Ruth coming to Bethlehem.' So, at the end of the chapter, at the city gate, the women flutter over Naomi.

But then you go to chapter two, and you have the barley field episode, and Ruth collects her ephah of barley, which is a good take. But notice what chapter two comes back to. Where's the focus? When Ruth returns with her ephah, the focus is on Naomi, who says, 'Blessed may he be by Yahweh who has not forsaken his steadfast love, et cetera, with the living or the dead.'

And then you go to the threshing floor episode in chapter three, and that's focused on Ruth and Boaz at the threshing floor, but then where does it end? Oh, it comes back at the end of chapter three to Naomi. Ruth comes in from the threshing floor and brings the measures of barley that Boaz sent home for her, and Ruth reports to Naomi – the chapter ends by focusing again on Naomi.

Then you go into chapter four, and you go to the courtroom scene, but where does that end up in verses 14 to 17? It comes back to Naomi. That's strange, because in chapter four you would think that after verse 13 the focus would be on Ruth and Boaz and their new little son .... But it's not.

It's on Naomi. It's as if the text is always bringing us back to focus on Naomi. Although it's not 'as if.' It does do that! Every chapter comes back to her. Every scene comes back to her. Oh, there are developments about Ruth and Boaz, true, but at the end of every episode the spotlight is on Naomi.

Now, that's a literary observation, you might say – but it has theological freight. What does it suggest? It suggests, doesn't it, that *Yahweh is preoccupied with Naomi's welfare?*

Do you know what preoccupation is? Well, the insides of pulpits, the parts a congregation doesn't normally see, are funny things. They can be filled with all kinds of junk that collects over the years. I remember one pulpit that stands out to me vividly. I was sitting down on the chancel of a church in Mississippi. I was preaching for a seminary student that Sunday, filling in for him in this country church, and in the pulpit there were two aerosol cans of wasp and hornet spray. And when I saw them, I wished I would have had those cans a little earlier in my ministry!

My first pastorate in Kansas, many moons ago, was what we call a two-point charge. We had a town church in a small town, and then another church in the country six miles south of the town. I would go out to the country church at 9:30 and preach, and then would come into the town church for the second service at 11:00.

I was out at this country church. You know what country churches can be like. They get shut up and heated during the winter, and then comes a little warmer weather closer to spring, like about May or so.

That's when things come to life a bit. Some of the pests that have been hibernating start waking up; especially wasps. (Though I don't know if they actually hibernate). I remember one Lord's Day I was preaching to this congregation from Jeremiah 31 on the new covenant. Only, I was having problems holding their attention because there were one or two wasps in there doing their thing. You know how graceful wasps can be.

The congregation was doing its best. They were really trying to look at me. So there are about fifty people and, whether they are really interested or not, they are actually making an effort to pay attention. But the wasps were making it very hard for them. As I would look them in the eye, I could see their eyes going all around as they watched the kamikaze wasps make their dives.

There was just nothing that anyone could do. They just were preoccupied with that wasp. At least, until the wasp made a mistake. He (or she?) landed right on the front of the pulpit, and I smacked him and flicked him onto the carpet below, and we were back in the new covenant again.

But they were just preoccupied. They were fixated on that wasp, and try as they might they simply couldn't get their attention off it. That's the way it is with Yahweh in the book of Ruth.

This pattern in which the attention always comes back to Naomi implies that she is never absent from Yahweh's mind. Naomi is never forgotten. She is ever and always the focus of Yahweh's attentions. It's as if Yahweh is preoccupied, as if he's fixated on her welfare and cannot let go of the matter. Faith can scarcely imagine the intensity of God's care.

Faith can seldom guess what God will do through affliction

That is our third proposition. Now this genealogy in verses 18 to 22 is really the most important part of the book. It's the climax of the book. Naomi's grandson, Obed, is a part of it all. Note that the genealogy in verse 18 leads up to David in the last of verse 22.

Now, David is the covenant king. Of course, that should turn your lights on a little bit because some of you have cheated and read ahead in the story, and you know that you eventually come to 2 Samuel 7. You know that there David is the king through whom Yahweh has promised to establish his kingdom in this world. You remember from 2 Samuel 7, perhaps, verses 12 to 16, that covenant that Yahweh made in which he makes three affirmations to David about his kingdom promise: that death does not annul it, that sin cannot destroy it, and that time will not exhaust it.

And even though that line of Davidic kings will go into eclipse to a certain degree and won't be visible, it's through David's line that Jesus the Messiah comes into the world.

Do you get it now? This story in the book of Ruth is not just a nice private family story, but it's an essential episode in the prime familial line of the kingdom of God.

So Naomi's story, with all its turmoil and angst and tears and trouble, is a contributing part of the story of the coming of God's kingdom. So much is hidden behind those brief words in verse 21, 'and Boaz fathered Obed' – but you know, because you've read this story, that behind that simple statement is packed all the heartache that Naomi endured. Everything Naomi – and Ruth – went through was part of what led up to the establishing of Yahweh's kingdom in this world, through his servant David in the imminent future, and eventually through his Son Jesus.

This is a perspective that Naomi could probably never see. Oh, I know in verses 11 and 12, there was a prayer that hoped and looked and asked for something greater like this, but this was something that Naomi, from her flat-footed position in her own sandals at that time, could have probably never guessed. Sometimes there are perspectives that we just can't imagine.

Warren Wiersbe, who was a pastor and a rather well-known Bible expositor, was telling of the time when he had gallbladder trouble. He had a terrific problem with his gallbladder, and finally had to go in and have it taken out. So sometime after his surgery he was waiting to get checked out of the hospital; finally his surgeon Dr Lloyd Tenney (who was a Christian) came into his room to sign him out.

Wiersbe said to Dr Tenney, 'You know, God gave me a gallbladder, and you took it out. Did God make a mistake?'

'Nope,' came Tenney's reply, as he continued to fill out the papers.

Wiersbe wasn't satisfied, and pressed on: 'If I can do without it, then why did God give it to me in the first place?'

To which Dr Tenney replied, 'So I can send my kids to college.'

Who would have ever had that in view? Who could have ever seen or guessed that perspective?

But that's just it, isn't it? How could Naomi have seen 150 years down the timeline, and see the kingship of David? How could Naomi have known that her affliction and her trouble would lead up to this covenant king who would offer Israel, through God's grace, a secure place, and eventually lead to the coming of God's own Son?

But in the perspective of the book of Ruth, the story of Naomi, seen in the light of this final genealogy, tells us that famine, and triple grief, and destitution, and the conversion of a Moabite girl, and barley fields, and threshing floors, and courtrooms, and the wail of little Obed coming out of the nursery, all of it, was the way God was in the process of establishing his kingdom on earth.

You may have heard about what *Progressive Farmer* magazine a few years ago called the 'Pest of Honor.' It's down in Enterprise, Alabama. If you don't live down there, you don't need to go there. It's hot there. But down in Enterprise, Alabama, they have a particular monument.

They had a problem there. Enterprise was a cotton-raising area, and sometime around 1910 the boll weevil came. And in about 1914, they produced 38,000 bales of cotton, but by 1917, only 7,000 bales of cotton. Farmers tried everything to get rid of those boll weevils. They tried picking them off and drowning them. They tried spraying them with carbolic acid, and they tried ashes, and they tried various insecticides – they even tried whiskey. But nothing worked.

So some of the fellows decided to find alternatives to cotton. Some of them turned to peanut farming and found that to be very profitable. Others turned to corn, hay, or livestock. And after a while, the farming economy stabilized, and the area began to prosper. So by about 1919, one of the men in town said, 'We ought to erect a monument.' And they did, although it didn't reach its final form until 1949.

But it's there in Enterprise, Alabama – a statuesque woman holding aloft a 17-and-a-half pound football-sized replica of a boll weevil made of iron. It was the Devastator that became their preserver, although no one could ever have guessed that at the time. Faith can seldom guess what God may do through affliction.

And the reason this is important is because it shows that none of us knows enough to say that God doesn't know what he's doing. None of us has enough wisdom to dispute God's strange ways, but we have enough clues from Naomi's story to show us that *God takes common and complicated circumstances in the lives of his people and makes them contribute to the coming of his kingdom in this world.*

Who is a God like you, Yahweh, who brings your blessing,
your care, and your wisdom into our dilapidated and
frazzled lives, who both maintains your kingdom and
holds your people in your steadfast love?
Praise be to you, O Lord!

Amen.

Christian Focus Publications

Our mission statement

Staying Faithful

In dependence upon God we seek to impact the world through literature faithful to His infallible Word, the Bible. Our aim is to ensure that the Lord Jesus Christ is presented as the only hope to obtain forgiveness of sin, live a useful life and look forward to heaven with Him.

Our Books are published in four imprints:

CHRISTIAN FOCUS

Popular works including biographies, commentaries, basic doctrine and Christian living.

MENTOR

Books written at a level suitable for Bible College and seminary students, pastors, and other serious readers. The imprint includes commentaries, doctrinal studies, examination of current issues and church history.

CHRISTIAN HERITAGE

Books representing some of the best material from the rich heritage of the church.

CF4KIDS

Children's books for quality Bible teaching and for all age groups: Sunday school curriculum, puzzle and activity books; personal and family devotional titles, biographies and inspirational stories – because you are never too young to know Jesus!

Christian Focus Publications Ltd,
Geanies House, Fearn, Ross-shire,
IV20 1TW, Scotland, United Kingdom.
www.christianfocus.com